STRATEGY FORMULATION

FOR
GENERAL MANAGERS
Second Edition

*a practical guide
for establishing
corporate strategy*

HENRY H. BEAM
Western Michigan University

 KENDALL/HUNT PUBLISHING COMPANY
2460 Kerper Boulevard P.O. Box 539 Dubuque, Iowa 52004-0539

Copyright © 1990, 1993 by Kendall/Hunt Publishing Company

Library of Congress Catalog Card Number: 92–74351

ISBN 0–8403–8203–0

Printed in the United States of America
10 9 8 7 6 5 4 3 2 1

CONTENTS

PREFACE

This book presents in one short volume what general managers should know about strategy formulation. By definition, a general manager looks at the organization as a whole, not simply at one aspect of it, or one functional specialty within it. Most individuals are hired because of their skill in a functional area such as accounting or marketing, not for their ability to think as a general manager. Yet after a few years with the company, they will find their chances for advancement are more closely tied to their ability to perform as a general manager, including the formulation and implementation of corporate strategy, than to their functional expertise. Accountants, engineers and other specialists will also benefit from knowledge of the basic concepts of strategy formulation. They will know what their bosses are talking about when they are asked to provide information for use in developing their organization's strategic plan.

Chapters 1 and 2 summarize the nature of the general manager's job and define and give examples of key strategic planning terms such as the mission statement. Chapter 3 develops a five-step strategic planning framework that can be used in a wide variety of situations. Chapters 4 and 5 then discuss the attractions and pitfalls of attempting to diversify. Chapter 6 discusses two popular approaches to managing diversified firms, the Boston Consulting Group (BCG) growth/share matrix and the General Electric/McKinsey Strategic Business Unit (SBU) concept.

Chapter 7 then relates strategy to the three basic ways to compete: price, quality, and service or delivery. It also explains some special ways to compete, such as patent protection or status (Patek Philippe and Rolex watches). The second addition includes a reading at the end of this chapter, "Strategic Discontinuities: When Being Good May Not be Enough." A firm is faced with a strategic discontinuity when a competitor finds a better way to provide the same goods or services, usually using a different way to compete. The final two chapters relate research and development and organizational structure to strategy.

I wrote this book because I felt there was a need for a text on strategic planning that was brief, readable and practical. I use this book as the text portion of the courses I teach in strategic management and combine it with one of the many good books of cases now available.

I owe a debt of gratitude to Tom Carey and Steve Hansen, my colleagues in the Department of Management, for encouraging me to write a short yet comprehensive and readable book on strategy formulation. Their comments were always helpful and to the point.

A special word of thanks goes to the many students who have provided helpful suggestions for this book. Their input is always welcome.

Henry H. Beam

— 1 —

THE PERSPECTIVE OF THE
GENERAL MANAGER

The job of the general manager is to integrate the functional activities (e.g., accounting, finance, marketing, production) of an organization into a unified program of action which will help achieve the organization's goals. In large organizations, these goals are usually made explicit as the strategic plan, which is the result of a strategic planning or strategy formulation process. Examples of general managers include both the sole proprietor of a local business and the chairman of a Fortune 500 firm such as General Electric, which in 1991 had annual sales of $60.2 billion, employed 284,000 people and produced thousands of different products from light bulbs to television sets to jet engines to financial services. Indeed, the head of any organization (business, government, military, university), regardless of its size, is by definition a *general manager*, and has strategic planning as one of his or her primary responsibilities.[1]

The jobs of the general manager and the functional specialist are both important, but are fundamentally different in two ways. First, the general manager should be concerned with all aspects of the business while the functional specialist should be concerned primarily with the performance of his own functional area. Second, there is a difference in the orientation toward data (including reports) between the general manager and the functional specialist. As shown in Exhibit 1.1, the functional departments are *preparers* of data while the general manager

---

1. Traditionally the head of a civilian organization was called its *president*, who reported to a board of directors which had its own *chairman*. Today the terms *chief executive officer* and *chief operating officer* are often used to describe the two top jobs. The responsibilities of the chief executive officer roughly parallel those of the chairman of the board and generally focus on *setting* strategy. The responsibilities of the chief operating officer roughly parallel those of the president, and generally focus on the implementation of strategy on a day to day basis. The military has used a similar assignment of responsibilities for many years. The commanding officer is in overall command (i.e., sets strategy or direction) while the executive officer, the next in command, implements the commanding officer's orders and policies. All of these individuals are general managers since they deal with the overall functioning of the organization rather than with only one or two functional areas.

is a *consumer* or *user* of that data. The general manager is responsible for integrating the data from all the functional areas and then making decisions that are in the best interests of the firm rather than favoring a single functional area at the expense of the firm as a whole.

Except in very small businesses (ten people or less), entry level managerial positions will be in a functional area rather than in general management. Indeed, most college graduates do start out working for large corporations, even if many of them later move to a small business or go into business for themselves. To get a job in a large corporation, it is necessary to have expertise (or the ability to gain it rapidly) in a functional specialty. However, to move up the ladder to jobs of greater responsibility which pay more money, a person needs to develop the perspective and skills of a general manager. This permits him or her to see beyond the narrow perspective of the functional specialist.

General managers are paid more than functional specialists (who often have more degrees) because their skills are harder to find. Thus John Delorean was paid $650,000 in 1972 when he ran the Chevrolet Division of General Motors. He had started his career twenty years earlier as a very capable engineer and designer, but those skills didn't get him the top job at Pontiac and later at Chevrolet, General Motors' largest division. He got those jobs, and was paid that much money, because of his skills as a general manager and his ability to motivate people in the functional areas to work for him.[2]

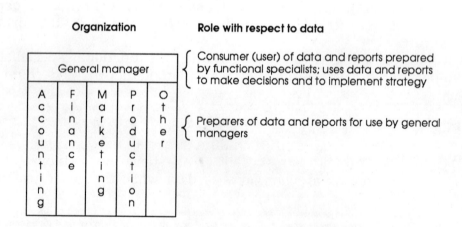

Exhibit 1.1. Roles with respect to data for general managers and functional specialists.

2. C. Rush Loving, "The Automobile Industry Has Lost Its Masculinity," *Fortune*, September 1973, p. 187.

THE THREE LEVELS OF MANAGEMENT

Management may be conveniently divided into three levels: top, middle and operating (also called supervisory or first line), as shown in Exhibit 1.2. The phrases "do things right" and "do the right things" are attributable to Peter Drucker.[3] What Drucker means by "do the right things" is that it is the responsibility of top management to make the right strategic decisions about what the firm should do in the future. If the wrong decision is made at the top, it matters little how well the rest of the organization functions. In the 1950s, the top management of Sperry Rand decided not to put major resources behind the Univac, the first commercially available computer, and a good one, too. As a result, Sperry Rand soon lost leadership of the market to IBM, which decided to go all out to become the leading firm in computers.

Operating management's responsibility is to "do things right." Those working on the shop floor weren't hired to think about the future of the company or new product ideas. Their task is to do their jobs as proficiently as they can, that is, "do things right." Indeed, each level has its own responsibilities and challenges, which we shall now review.

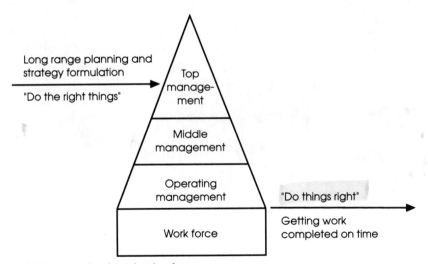

Exhibit 1.2. The three levels of management.

---

3. Peter F. Drucker, *The Practice of Management* (New York: Harper & Row, 1954). This is still one of the best books on the job of the general manager, even though it was published over thirty years ago.

3

Operating Management

The primary characteristic of the operating manager (sometimes called a first line supervisor), is that he or she does not perform the work personally, but is responsible for accomplishing the work through direct supervision of the efforts of others. Thus responsibility for work accomplishment is separated from technical proficiency in performing the work. Familiar operating management positions are factory foreman, Army second lieutenant, and bank branch manager. The primary focus is on accomplishing today's tasks. The key skills are dealing with people on a day to day basis and a technical understanding of the work to be accomplished. Planning is a small portion of the job and is usually related to scheduling work for the next few days or weeks. The desired result is on time delivery of current orders.

Middle Management

A middle manager is one who supervises other managers rather than members of the work force. Middle managers, who may be arrayed in several layers in large corporations, are at least one step away from members of the work force who do the actual work. Thus they are more isolated from day-to-day happenings than are operating managers.

For many years, large U.S. corporations such as General Motors and U.S. Steel operated with ten or more layers of management. In the 1980s, large corporations realized that to respond more quickly to competitive threats from abroad, they needed to eliminate many layers of management. As a result, there may be only half as many middle management jobs today as there were just two decades ago.

The planning horizon of middle managers is usually three months to a year. Middle managers may also have some budget authority, but their prime responsibility will be to work within budget rather than to set the budget.

Top Management

The chairman, president and vice-presidents constitute top management. Usually the status symbols of the office will tell you who is a member of top management: carpeted corner office with a nice view, a personal secretary, a title on the door and use of the executive dining room.[4] The primary task of top management is planning for the future of the

---

4. This is not always so. Some firms deliberately try to play down visible status differences between top management and the workers. Such firms may have no reserved parking spots except for visitors, no executive dining room, and expect all employees (including the chairman) to be called by their first name. Even though its sales in 1991 were over $40 billion, Wal-Mart still has its headquarters in a converted warehouse in Bentonville, Arkansas, and stresses a ''no frills'' approach to management throughout the organization.

organization. The planning horizon for top management is typically three to five years in most industrial firms. In some businesses, such as apparel, the planning horizon may be less than a year to accommodate the unpredictability of changes in fashion. In other businesses, such as pharmaceuticals, the planning horizon will be ten years or more because of the lengthy process involved in bringing a drug product to market after its discovery in the laboratory.

While these three categories are by no means exact, they do provide a useful way to look at the development of a person from functional specialist to generalist as he or she moves up the corporate ladder, including accepting a greater responsibility for strategic planning. However, these categories do not explicitly account for the large number of people in recent years who have taken staff positions in research and development, accounting or finance where their pay and status more nearly correspond to middle managers than to entry level operating managers.[5]

THE VIEW FROM THE TOP

The corporation may be considered analogous to a tall pyramid located in a large valley. A person proceeding up one side of the pyramid has a clear view of the valley behind him or her, but doesn't know how the valley looks from the other sides of the pyramid. Only upon arrival at the top is the whole valley plainly visible.

A similar situation exists in business. Let the sides of the pyramid represent the functional specialties of a business such as engineering, finance, marketing and production. A person advancing in one of these specialties tends to see problems and their importance in terms of his or her own specialty. Only when a person reaches the top (i.e., becomes a general manager) does he or she see the full picture. At this level, problems in one functional specialty should not be considered in isolation. Rather, they should be considered in relationship to problems in the other functional specialties so decisions can be made that are in the best interest of the organization as a whole, not just of one functional specialty.

5. For a still timely discussion of the pros and cons of starting in a staff position, see J. Sterling Livingston, "Myth of the Well Educated Manager," *Harvard Business Review*, January-February 1971, pp. 79–89. Also see Henry H. Beam, "Getting to the Top in Today's Business Environment," *Human Resource Management*, Summer 1978, pp. 24–28. For a discussion of the job of the general manager, see Andrall E. Pearson, "Six Basics for General Managers," *Harvard Business Review*, July–August 1989, pp. 94–101.

SUMMARY

This book deals with strategic planning from the point of view of top management. However, strategic planning is not solely the domain of top management. Middle and operating managers should also be familiar with the concepts of strategic planning since they are the ones who will be charged with implementing the strategic plan once it has been formulated. Accountants, engineers and other specialists can also benefit from knowledge of the basic concepts of strategic planning. Such knowledge will help them better understand the wishes of their bosses when they are asked to provide information for use in developing their organization's strategic plan.

—2—

THE VOCABULARY OF STRATEGIC PLANNING

Strategic planning, like any other field, has its own vocabulary. Managers should know this vocabulary since it greatly facilitates planning and communication, and hence effectiveness, in the organization. While the meaning of most terms is straightforward, some terms (e.g., mission statement) are not commonly used outside of top management. The purpose of this chapter is to provide working definitions of seven basic terms commonly used in strategic planning and to show how they relate to each other.

In defining and discussing these strategic planning terms, we will proceed from the general to the specific, starting with the most general of the seven terms first, the *mission statement*, and concluding with the most specific, a *procedure*.

THE MISSION STATEMENT

The *mission statement* (sometimes called the statement of corporate purpose) states the basic long term goals and objectives of a corporation or organization: what this organization desires to do on an ongoing basis.[1] The mission statement should answer the question, "What are we in business for in the long run?" It is better if it is explicit (written down), but it may also be implicit (derived from the firm's behavior). The mission statement should be neither too broad ("our purpose is to make a profit" or "our purpose is to survive") nor too narrow ("our business is to make steam locomotives and nothing else"). Exhibit 2.1 gives some well stated mission statements.

---

1. See, for example, R. Duane Ireland and Michael A. Hitt, "Mission Statements: Importance, Challenge and Recommendations for Development," *Business Horizons* (May–June 1992), pp. 34–42.

Organization	Mission Statement	Comment
Fire department	To save lives and protect property.	Unchanged for centuries.
Avis Rent-a-Car	To rent vehicles without drivers	Specific expertise in a segment of the transportation field.
IBM	To solve the informational needs of its customers.	Not dependent on a specific technology such as computers.
Abbott Laboratories	To provide health care world-wide.	Clearly stated and easy to understand.
McDonald's	To provide high quality, inexpensive fast food to the public.	Mission statement for a highly successful service firm.
Telephone Company	To provide superior communication services to the public.	Clear and to the point.
Scott Paper	To provide high quality paper products to consumers.	Clearly stated, yet allows for a wide range of products.
Brinks, Inc.	We move money.	Self-explanatory.
Cedar Point	Provide quality entertainment at reasonable prices to people of all ages.	What an amusement park should do.
Keebler Foods	To make uncommonly good cookies and crackers.	They do, too.

Exhibit 2.1. Examples of mission statements.

The mission statement is often as useful for what it does not say as for what it does say. In the case of the fire department and IBM, the customer's need is clearly identified (protection from fire, solving customer's informational needs), but the means of fulfilling that need are not. The mission statement of the fire department has not changed for centuries. Meanwhile, the technology to fight fires has progressed from bucket brigades and hand pumped, horse drawn fire engines in the early 1800s to today's modern gasoline powered fire engines, which can pump 20,000 gallons per minute from a city's fire mains. Similarly IBM's mission statement does not tie it to the computer as a way of satisfying customer needs, although most people naturally think of computers when they hear IBM mentioned. Indeed, prior to World War II (and before the invention of the computer), IBM was the largest supplier of tabulating systems and electric typewriters, products that solved the informational needs of its customers at that time.[2]

---

2. "International Business Machines," *Fortune*, November 1940, p. 36. Until the mid-1950s *Fortune* was printed monthly in a large (11" x 14") format and frequently contained comprehensive articles on leading corporations that are still interesting and informative.

The mission statement can be viewed as a watershed or dividing line for what endeavors a particular company should or should not undertake. Thus a telephone company with a mission statement "to provide superior communications services to the public" would logically invest in communication satellites and research in fiber optics as potentially better ways to carry high density messages. However, it would not logically make nuclear submarines for the Navy or develop new breakfast products for children. Rather than specialize in a particular type of product, some firms specialize in products related to a common theme or technology. The implicit mission statement of Minnesota Mining and Manufacturing (3M) Company is to "apply coatings to surfaces." This statement helps us to see the commonality between such seemingly unrelated products as scotch tape, Post-it note pads, furnace filters, film, Scotchgard fabric protector, flight deck coverings for aircraft carriers, video tape and sandpaper (the firm's original product).

A well thought out mission statement should not need to be changed very often. It should provide overall guidance for the firm's operations, including what new products to develop or businesses to enter, but it should not be so broad as to be a mere platitude. On the other hand, it should not be so narrow that it needs to be changed to accommodate every new technological development or competitive threat the firm faces. If you considered yourself to be in the snow *shoveling* business, you would be restricting yourself to only one way of removing snow. By restating your mission to be snow *removal*, it would be consistent for you to remove snow not only by shoveling, but also by using a snowblower or a plow, or possibly some method that didn't involve scraping at all, such as utilizing salt or an electric current to melt it. But be careful not to make your definition too broad. If you defined your business as cleaning surfaces, then you could also reasonably be asked to wash cars, clean windows and scrub carpets as well as remove snow—tasks you may neither want to do nor be equipped to do, even if they are consistent with your mission statement.

If you have trouble developing a mission statement that relates concisely to the business's products or services, it may be that the mission statement relates more to how the product or service is provided. Thus Tandy Corporation can be viewed as a *distributor* of the products of technology (electronics components for hobbyists through its Radio Shack division, computers through its Tandy division) rather than a *maker* of them. The products Tandy distributes may change (audio components in the 1960s, CB radios in the 1970s, cellular phones in the 1980s), but its implicit mission statement as "the leading distributor of the products of electronics technology" does not.

In general, a well stated mission statement should be independent of the technology used to accomplish it, but should not be so broad or generic as to include activities in which the firm is clearly not interested. An exception is when the company itself deliberately elects to feature a specific technology. This is often true of businesses which deliberately try to identify what they do in their name, such as Gene's Steam Cleaning, Kentucky Fried Chicken or Snap-On Tools.

STRATEGY

Strategy is the determination of the broad courses of action and allocation of resources necessary to accomplish the organizational purpose or mission statement. The word "strategy" comes from the Greek *strategia*, which means the art of generalship, and that is the sense in which it is used here. Robert Wood, President of Sears Roebuck and Company from 1928 to 1954 when it became American's largest retailer, captured the essence of strategy: "Business is like war in one respect. If its grand strategy is correct, any number of tactical errors can be made and yet the enterprise proves successful."[3]

Discussions of strategy often include references to military battles and wars, partly because the military has studied strategy for centuries. Many countries have advanced military institutions (e.g., our Naval War College in Newport, Rhode Island) devoted to the study of military strategy and related topics. Most high ranking officers spend a year or more at such institutions during their careers.[4]

Athletics also provide well known examples of different strategies. The layman's term for strategy, the "game plan," originated in football and has been carried over into business and politics. Athletic contests provide excellent examples of the virtues and shortcomings of various strategies in light of each team's or participant's resources and skills. Thus in football we may see a running team versus a passing team; in tennis a baseliner versus a serve and volleyer; and in baseball the patience of the hit and run versus swinging for the fences and the instant payoff of the home run.

Strategies may be oriented toward beating a competitor, as General Motors versus Ford in automobiles or Apple versus IBM in personal

---

3. Alfred D. Chandler, Jr., *Strategy and Structure* (Cambridge, MA: MIT Press, 1962), p. 235.

4. A case in point is five-star General Omar Bradley. In his autobiography he recounted that over half his first twenty-three years of service after graduating from West Point in 1915 had been spent either as a student or an instructor in Army schools. This was also true of many of Bradley's contemporaries, including Dwight D. Eisenhower and George C. Marshall. See Omar Bradley and Clay Blair, *A General's Life* (New York: Simon and Schuster, 1983), p. 79.

computers. Or they may be oriented toward benefitting from scientific developments, as was the case with Xerox in the development of plain paper copiers and Polaroid in the development of instant photography. But as new discoveries are exploited and inventions perfected, business strategies will inevitably be played out against the external competitors that are sure to enter the field. Such competition may be broad based, including products which can substitute for each other as well as among firms making the same product. Aluminum and plastic compete with steel for use in new cars, and natural gas competes with electricity (and more recently, solar power) to heat the hot water in people's homes. Thus the set of possible strategic alternatives for a firm should be broadly enough conceived to account for all reasonable possibilities, including likely technological developments and actions of competitors.

In terms of time, changes in strategy are apt to occur more frequently than changes in the mission statement. This is because strategy is often closely tied to the technology that is available when it is formulated. The electronics industry in particular is characterized by rapid technological change, and the strategy of a firm in this industry is likely to change as the technology changes. However, in the automobile industry, strategies have changed little for over fifty years. Gaining market share to take advantage of economies of scale in production continues to be the basic strategy of all large automobile companies.

OBJECTIVES AND GOALS

The terms *objective* and *goal* are virtually synonymous.[5] Both refer to a desired future state which, ideally, is definable and measurable. Objectives or goals have inherent in them the need for measurement; hence they are more specific than either the mission statement or strategy, neither of which has measurement inherent in it. Objectives also explicitly introduce the dimension of time, since by definition an objective should be attainable at some specified future time. Often each unit or organization will have objectives for a specific period of time, such as one or two years.

Examples of objectives are given in Exhibit 2.2. Note that each of these examples is specific enough with respect to measurement so that it is possible to tell when the objective has been obtained or what progress has been made toward its attainment. To be meaningful, objectives

---

5. While some management theorists make a distinction between goals and objectives, they are considered synonymous in this discussion. If a distinction in usage is made (e.g., goals refer to items that are longer term in nature, objectives refer to items that are shorter term in nature, or vice-versa), it is less important what the distinction is than that it is maintained consistently throughout the organization. For a discussion of these terms, see Anthony Raia, *Managing by Objectives* (New York: Scott, Foresman, 1974).

Unit/Organization	Objective
Retailer	Open thirty new outlets nationwide each year.
R & D	Develop three new products in the next two years.
Marketing	Obtain 10% market share for a new consumer product in three years.
Manufacturing	Keep defects to less than 5%. Keep scrap rate to less than 10%.
Personnel	Keep absenteeism below 3% for the year. Keep turnover below 10% per year.
Football team	Win the conference championship within three years.
Tennis player	Don't double fault more than once per set.

Exhibit 2.2. Examples of objectives.

should be challenging, but should not be so difficult as to be virtually unattainable.

PLANS, PROGRAMS AND PROJECTS

A *plan* is a specific course of action, generally for a subunit of the organization, for which resources have been allocated for a designated period of time, such as a year. In essence, a plan adds budget responsibility to an objective or goal. Since most budgets are adopted for a period of a year or less, most plans are also for a year or less. However, exceptions may occur, as in the drug industry, where it routinely takes ten years or more to bring new products to market, or in the forest products business, an extreme case, where it may take a hundred years to grow a new stand of timber.

A *program* is closely related to a plan. The primary difference is that a plan usually has a shorter time span associated with it, often a year or less, while a program has a considerably longer, perhaps indefinite, duration. For example, a retailing firm may undertake a program (which will last several years) for building stores in new locations. A major Kmart program of the 1980s was to open medium sized stores in hitherto uncovered regionally attractive locations, such as Bad Axe in the heart of Michigan's thumb. Or a college may place stronger emphasis on its basketball program, including recruiting, expecting to see a significant improvement in its team, and also have a plan to build a new field house for its games.

At any given time a large organization will very likely have several programs in various stages of implementation. One of the main tasks of

strategic planing is to ensure that all of a company's plans and programs are consistent with both its mission statement and its strategy. A
special type of plan is a *contingency plan*, which will only be placed in
effect if undesired or unexpected events occur. Most organizations and
communities have well developed contingency plans for emergencies or
disasters, such as flooding, tornados or power shortages.

A *project* may be defined as a special type of plan where the dates
for starting and completing each task associated with it are specified
only relative to each other and not to calendar dates. Most firms (and
individuals, too) have many projects they would like to see accomplished, but lack the time, resources or motivation to get them done.
Technically a project becomes a plan when it is assigned a starting
date, thus automatically associating completion dates with each of the
tasks associated with it. But this distinction often becomes blurred in
practice. For example, in construction and research and development
it is common to speak of project management. The person in charge is
referred to as the project manager, and has overall responsibility for
resources which are frequently drawn from different functional areas
of the organization.

Projects are temporary by nature. When the project is completed, the
project organization is usually dissolved and the resources either returned to their source departments or reassigned to other projects. Well
known examples of successful large projects are the Manhattan Project
during World War II to build the atomic bomb, the Polaris submarine
project during the late 1950s to build the Fleet Ballistic Missile (FBM)
submarines, and project Apollo of the 1960s to land a man on the moon
by 1969. Plans, programs and projects are similar to objectives in that
they all have measurement inherent in them and specify what is to be
done and when. However, they differ in that plans, programs and projects also make provision for allocation of resources (i.e., budget authority), while objectives do not. The time dimension of a plan, a project or
an objective is generally from a few months (i.e., a quarter) to a few
years, while a program usually covers a considerably longer period of
time due to its ongoing or recurring nature.

POLICY

The term *policy* has two distinct meanings depending on the context in
which it is used. First, it is used to specify the actions the top decision
makers in the organization will take with regard to other organizations. In
this context, policy may be considered a synonym for strategy formulated

at the highest levels. This high level use of the word policy occurs frequently in government, which deals primarily with external entities. Thus the President may speak of the country's foreign policy, economic policy or defense policy.

Second, policy is used to specify what guidelines should apply or what actions should be taken by individuals within the organization in response to issues of a non-strategic nature. In this context, policy is a guide to action which can be thought out in advance. Policies can then be implemented on a consistent basis by personnel at lower levels in the organization. Most retailers now have a policy of giving cash refunds for all purchases when the customer provides a sales slip and returns the merchandise in good condition. The value of this policy is that it allows entry level employees to make a wide variety of decisions promptly without seeking approval by the store manager. The store manager is thus free to concentrate on the job he is paid to perform, namely the overall operation of the store.

However, a policy by definition has some flexibility inherent in it. It is simply a guide to action which can be applied quickly, consistently and simply to the vast majority of situations which are routine in nature. If circumstances warrant, the person responsible for implementing the policy is expected to override it. Unusually large or frequent returns may merit calling the store manager to insure that the spirit of the policy isn't being violated, or that stolen merchandise isn't being returned for a cash refund.

The major advantage of a set of policies is that it promotes efficiency by permitting the vast majority of decisions to be carried out at the lowest possible level unless unusual circumstances dictate otherwise. A well thought out set of policies can greatly facilitate the smooth functioning of an organization. Exhibit 2.3 gives some familiar examples of policies for

Situation	Policy
Bank	Don't cash checks for people without an account.
Building lobby	No loitering or soliciting.
Restaurant	First come, first served.
Tickets to concerts or athletic events	Last year's season ticket holders have first priority.
Retail store	Satisfaction guaranteed or your money back.
Photography studio	Can't take a portrait out of the studio without a $50 deposit.

Exhibit 2.3. Examples of policies for customers.

Functional Area	Policy
Finance	Increase the dividend each year.
	Pay approximately fifty percent of net income out as dividends.
Management	Promote only from within.
Personnel	Transfer employees to a different unit when they are promoted.
Production	Plant manager can approve purchase orders up to $5,000.
Purchasing	Obtain at least three bids on each item procured.
	Buy from local suppliers, other factors being equal.
	Pay all bills within thirty days of receipt.

Exhibit 2.4. Examples of policies in businesses.

customers, and Exhibit 2.4 gives examples of policies in functional areas of a business.

General Motors has long had a policy of promoting managers only from within. All top line and finance staff managers for the past sixty years have been promoted from within. However, when General Motors has needed individuals with specific expertise to head certain staff functions, it has not hesitated to override the promote from within policy. Dr. Robert Forsch, a former top NASA administrator, was hired to head Research and Development; Dr. Stephen Fuller, Dean of Harvard's School of Business, was brought in to be Vice-President of Personnel; and Dr. Marina Whitman, formerly a member of the President's Council of Economic Advisers, was made the corporation's Chief Economist and a Vice-President.

Policies should be consistent with both an organization's mission statement and its strategy, and should be simply stated. In terms of the time dimension, policies are more apt to change quickly than either an organization's mission statement or its strategy. Occasionally a policy may become part of a firm's strategy. Historically, Sears used its policy of "satisfaction guaranteed or your money back" to develop a large, loyal customer base.

Policies are not an end in themselves, and should be reviewed periodically to see if they need to be updated or eliminated. If policies are allowed to proliferate, they can lead to rigidity, inflexibility and loss of efficiency in the organization. For example, in 1970, the Dana Corporation, a Toledo, Ohio, based maker of auto and truck parts, decided to change its rigid, highly centralized organization to a "paperless people involvement" form which delegated most daily operating decisions to the divisions. At the same time, it replaced its detailed, three inch thick corporate policies and procedures manual with a one page statement of policy.[6]

PROCEDURE

A *procedure* is a specific way to carry out a task. Examples of procedures abound in everyday life: making coffee, balancing a checkbook, running a computer program, or tying a knot. Policies and procedures are often considered to be nearly synonymous, as in a company's policies and procedures manual. However, there is a difference. A policy provides guidance on *what* to do while a procedure tells *how* to do it. Thus a policy tells whether an employee is eligible for reimbursement for travel expenses, while a procedure tells how to fill out the travel claim per se.

A procedure requires no discretion or understanding of the underlying phenomenon on the part of the person carrying it out, only an ability to follow instructions. Thus a procedure is efficient because it permits people to use such familiar items as a car, camcorder or television set with only a cursory understanding of how they really work. The disadvantage of a procedure is that it is inflexible. There may be errors in the procedure, or the procedure may no longer be applicable. But most people would have no way of knowing this, and even if they did, they would be at a loss to know what corrective action to take. Being able to drive a car, use a camcorder or operate a compact disc (CD) player is not synonymous with being able to fix one of these technologically sophisticated devices if something goes wrong with it.

In summary, a procedure tells how to perform a specific task but does not tell whether, by whom, why or when it should be performed. And it provides no guidance on how to take corrective action if an error is encountered.

RULES AND REGULATIONS

Rules and *regulations* are specific statements which tell what can and cannot be done by an organization or by individuals working in it. Rules and regulations may not have the force of law, but repeated violations of rules may be sufficient grounds for dismissal, as in persistent unexcused

---

6. Charles H. Gibson, "Paperless People Involvement-Management Philosophy at the Dana Corporation," *S.A.M. Advanced Management Journal*, Summer 1975, p. 6.

absences from work.[7] Rules and regulations may apply to the organization as a whole (e.g., regulation of the rate structure of public utilities by state regulatory agencies) or to individuals (e.g., safety precautions which must be followed; limited access to certain records or spaces).

Changes in rules and regulations should be infrequent. Unlike policies, which permit flexibility if circumstances warrant, rules and regulations should apply to everyone all the time. Any contradictions should be worked out to prevent ambiguity over which rule or regulation should take precedence.

If people never made mistakes or never exercised poor judgment, rules would not be necessary. In fact, when a new rule is promulgated in an organization, chances are it is the result of a problem that required top management attention to resolve. Some organizations, such as the U.S. Navy, have so many rules and regulations it is virtually impossible for a person to know them all and have time left over to do his or her job. Thus some rules are probably always necessary, but too many rules can also have a negative impact on an organization's ability to function.

Some organizations consider rules to be very desirable. Unions strive to have work rules clearly stated: who can do what kind of work and under what circumstances. But carried to an extreme, work rules can make an organization too rigid and inadvertently reduce its overall efficiency.

SUMMARY

This set of definitions of seven basic strategic planning terms has proceeded from the general to the specific. There are two reasons for this. First, this accommodates a logical and consistent translation of *time invariant* statements such as the mission statement to *time specific* statements such as those found in plans and programs. In fact, a time dimension is implicit in four of the terms:

The Mission Statement

Should be largely time invariant, and except in exceptional circumstances, should change only slowly with time. In the case of the fire department, the mission statement hasn't changed for centuries.

---

7. In some jobs, such as flying an airplane, performing surgery, or operating a nuclear reactor, it is extremely important to follow rules and regulations precisely since a mistake may be fatal. It may be necessary to obtain a license in addition to extensive professional training before starting work on such jobs.

Strategy

Must take into account certain time dependent events. Thus in formulating strategy, a firm such as General Motors needs to take into account events such as World War II which caused great changes in its production priorities during the war. Similarly, at the end of the war, General Motors had to change its priorities once again to producing primarily consumer goods such as automobiles.[8]

An Objective

Should have a date for attainment included in it. Thus Firm A may have an objective of completing its new research and development center by the end of next year.

Plans, Programs and Projects

These often have specific timetables included with them. They may make use of such planning devices as a Gantt or PERT chart to provide a time sequencing of the events required for their accomplishment.[9]

The remaining terms—*policies, rules and regulations* and *procedures*—are meant to be time independent, but need to be reviewed periodically to insure that they are still applicable.

Second, these terms represent the process whereby values are translated into actions.[10] The mission statement represents the summation of value judgments by those at the top of the organization as to what the organization should do. There are no limits to corporate endeavors, except that corporations, like people, are prohibited by law from doing anything that is illegal. Thus it is a value judgment as to what the corporation *should* do, that is, what its mission statement will be. A value is "good" or "bad" only in light of the value structure of the person doing the evaluating. However, personal values may come into conflict with the values of the organization. Stanley Kresge, son of the founder of the S.S. Kresge Company, now Kmart Corporation, did not drink alcoholic beverages for religious reasons. He became so upset when Kmart began selling beer and wine in its stores in 1985 that he sold most the 885,000 shares

---

8. These transitions are described in Peter F. Drucker's case study of General Motors, *The Concept of the Corporation* (New York: Mentor, 1964). The original version was published in 1947.

9. PERT stands for Program Evaluation Review Technique. PERT was developed in the late 1950s by the management consulting firm of Booz Allen and Hamilton for the Special Projects Office of the U.S. Navy as an aid in managing the Polaris missile and submarine programs.

10. For a discussion of values and facts related to decision making, see Herbert A. Simon, *Administrative Behavior*, third edition (New York: MacMillan, 1976). Simon received the Nobel prize for economics in 1978 for his contributions to the field of decision making, many of which were originally stated in the first edition of this book in 1947.

he owned in the company. As far as Kmart Corporation was concerned, Mr. Kresge's actions "are his own business. We put in our stores what our customers want."[11]

After working through strategy and objectives, we are ready for plans and programs. These are factual statements of actions that are planned in advance, and may include one or more projects to be accomplished. We can use standard methods of engineering, finance and accounting to determine if the plans and programs have been accomplished as scheduled. These are questions of fact, and may be evaluated as being correct or incorrect (i.e., was the plan accomplished on time?).

Thus the vocabulary of strategic planing may also be viewed as translating questions of value into questions of fact. This is a very powerful accomplishment. It provides a link of logic and consistency between the workers on the shop floor who are interested in getting today's work done (efficiency) and its top managers who are (or should be) concerned primarily with the corporation's purpose and its strategy (effectiveness).

---

11. "Principle Sale," *The Wall Street Journal*, May 22, 1985, p. 35.

— 3 —
A STRATEGIC PLANNING FRAMEWORK

Since the 1960s, strategic planning has emphasized the development of sophisticated planning techniques to deal with the increased diversity of today's large businesses. However, such advanced techniques as portfolio planning models are fully applicable only to the largest, most diversified firms.[1] In contrast, general managers in firms of all sizes have a large and ongoing need for a straightforward approach to strategic planning on the unit level, whether that unit is a division (or product line) of a large firm or the firm itself, as in the case of single product firms and most medium-sized and small businesses. The purpose of this chapter is to present a versatile, yet comprehensive, strategic planning framework that can be used by all general managers regardless of the size of their organization.

VIEWPOINT OF A STRATEGIC ANALYSIS

The viewpoint assumed in a strategic analysis is always that of top management. By definition this viewpoint is integrative in nature and does not favor a particular functional area of the business. A consequence of this viewpoint is that conducting a strategic analysis differs fundamentally from solving a problem of a quantitative nature, both in the way it is approached and in the nature of the solution itself.

When solving a quantitative problem, the objective is to find the right answer by selecting the correct formula and doing the appropriate calculations. In contrast, when solving a business strategy problem, the

---

1. Portfolio planning models were developed to help very diversified firms (e.g., Textron, General Electric) determine which divisions to keep and which to divest, much the way an investor would manage a portfolio of stocks. These models are discussed in Chapter 6. The strategic planning framework presented in this chapter is fully compatible with portfolio planning models since it may be applied to each business unit within the portfolio to develop an appraisal of that unit or a strategy for it.

objective is to analyze a set of strategic alternatives and select (or recommend) one for implementation. Occasionally one of the strategic alternatives under consideration will be clearly preferable to the others, but it is much more common to have different strategic alternatives rank high on different criteria. This complicates the problem of choosing among alternatives. The choice and weighting of decision criteria, the actions of competitors, the situation itself, and the values and goals of those involved in making the decision are just some of the factors which should be taken into account when evaluating strategic alternatives.

While the correctness of an answer to a problem of a quantitative nature can be demonstrated mathematically, no such check is possible for the recommended solution to a problem in business strategy. The best that the analyst can do is to ensure that the alternative recommended is *logical* and *consistent* in light of the information available and the goals and values of those making the final decision.

In addition, the business entity and its environment are in a continual process of interaction and change, and the effectiveness of a particular strategy may change dramatically with time.

CONSIDER the automobile industry. When gasoline was inexpensive in the 1950s and 1960s (about thirty cents a gallon), automobile companies achieved great success by building large cars with high horsepower, fuel inefficient engines. When the Arab oil embargo of 1973 caused the price of a gallon of gasoline to soar to well over dollar a gallon, such a strategy lost its effectiveness as customers began placing a premium on fuel efficiency. During the 1970s all major U.S. automakers changed their strategy to offer lighter, smaller and more fuel efficient cars.[2]

Strategic decisions tend to be time sensitive. Hence they frequently have to be made before all the pertinent facts can be obtained. This means that *realistic assumptions* may need to be made about data and variables that are not known but are critical to the analysis, such as estimates of future rates of inflation or a competitor's likely response to a particular strategy. Once made, a realistic assumption is treated as a fact for purposes of planning. Should it become evident that a realistic assumption is incorrect, part or all of the analysis will probably need to be redone.

Sometimes there is the opposite problem as well: having too much data. Unlimited amounts of data could be gathered about most strategic

---

2. Joseph Kraft, "Annals of Industry: The Downsizing Decision," *The New Yorker*, May 5, 1980, pp. 134–162.

business situations. But opportunities may pass if too much time is spent gathering data. Thus a very important task in the formulation of strategy is to determine which facts and opinions are pertinent to the analysis, which can be discarded as irrelevant, and which are missing. The strategist then makes realistic assumptions as necessary about unknown aspects of the situation so the analysis can proceed in a timely fashion. Hence the starting point for a strategic analysis of a business situation is the selection of a set of premises, that is, those facts, opinions and realistic assumptions that are pertinent to the situation.

The methodology of the business strategist is analogous to that of the physician. Just as the physician recommends a treatment based on what he knows about the patient, so too the business strategist recommends a course of action based on what he knows about a particular situation at the time he has to make a decision. The physician and the business strategist both must be knowledgeable in their fields. For both, the real measure of competence is the ability to go beyond the acquisition of knowledge per se to its application to specific situations, including those where some pertinent facts are missing or may never be known.

THE FIVE STEP STRATEGIC PLANNING FRAMEWORK

The strategic planning framework consists of five basic steps and is summarized in Exhibit 3.1. The five steps need not be carried out in order, but they should all be covered if the analysis is to be comprehensive in nature.

STEP I.
WHERE IS OUR COMPANY NOW?

The answer to this question consists of two parts: an external analysis of the environment and an internal evaluation of the firm's strengths and weaknesses.

A. External Analysis

What threats or opportunities face the firm?

Threats to a firm's current products can arise from obsolescence from technological breakthroughs, new competitors, or changed environmental conditions.

I. Where is our company now?

External analysis: look at the environment to identify:

- risks or threats
- opportunities
- competitors

Internal analysis: look inside the organization to identify:

- strengths
- weaknesses

• use ratio analysis to assess financial health and to determine any financial problems, constraints or strengths

II. What trends do we see?

- can we project the time of development?
- what effect might the trend(s) have on our company?

III. What are we in business for? What is our mission statement or statement of corporate purpose?

IV. What are our strategic alternatives (courses of action to attain our goals as derived from our mission statement)?

- We can always keep doing what we have been doing (no change)
- Keep the number of alternatives suggested to four or five to facilitate analysis

V. Select the best strategic alternative for implementation:

- Weigh each strategic alternative against the mission statement and relevant criteria
- Suggested criteria for evaluating strategic alternatives:

  ° Suitability: will this strategic alternative accomplish our goals?

  ° Feasibility: do we have the resources available to implement this strategic alternative?

  ° Acceptability: will this strategic alternative be acceptable to all parties concerned? Personal values should be considered here as well as any legal or ethical considerations.

  ° Risk: is the degree of risk associated with the alternative acceptable to all concerned?

Exhibit 3.1. Framework for solving business strategy problems.

IN 1960 there were seemingly unlimited uses for vacuum tubes in such growth markets as radio, radar, color television and computers. However, sales of vacuum tubes peaked in 1965 and decreased steadily every year thereafter. This should not have been a surprise. The transistor, a solid state device that was smaller and less expensive than the vacuum tube but performed much better in most applications, had been invented in 1947 at the Bell Telephone Laboratories. The transistor was soon threatening the supremacy of the vacuum tube as the basic electronic building block. Within two decades, sales of transistors had surpassed those of vacuum tubes, which were largely relegated to the replacement market.

IN THE 1980s home video recorders (camcorders), which feature instant viewing on a television set, ease of editing and reusable videotape, brought sales of home movie cameras to a virtual standstill.

Opportunities often arise from problems or from unfulfilled needs, as these examples show:

HENRY J. KAISER, noted industrialist of the 1930s through the 1950s, frequently remarked that "problems are opportunities in work clothes." During World War II there was an immediate need for more merchant ships. Even though he had no experience in shipbuilding, Kaiser looked on this problem as an opportunity, applied the construction industry techniques he was familiar with to shipbuilding (his firm had built Hoover Dam), and by the end of the war his firm alone was completing Liberty ships at the rate of one a day. Largely due to Kaiser's innovations, the United States as a country built 5,330 ships during the four years of the war, an average of over four ships *per day.*

RAY KROC, the founder of McDonald's, saw that the American penchant for hamburgers together with the development of a nationwide network of expressways provided the ideal opportunity for a chain of clean, conveniently located, moderately priced fast food restaurants. The first McDonald's opened on April 15, 1955 in Des Plaines, Illinois. By 1990 over 70 billion McDonald's hamburgers had been sold, a clear tribute to Kroc's good business sense.[3]

3. For the complete story of McDonald's, see John F. Love, *McDonald's: Behind the Arches* (New York: Bantam Books, 1986). The original McDonald Brothers restaurant, which gave Kroc his idea for the McDonald's chain, was located in San Bernadino, California, on one of the country's first major freeways. Motorists (and motorcyclists, too) appreciated a clean restaurant where they could get good food at a reasonable price in a short period of time.

■■■■■ For the first half of this century, strip mines along the Monongahela River provided coal for Pittsburgh's steel mills. Once the mining was completed, the land was considered worthless. Then in 1975, Bill Ford, a local businessman, purchased some of this land, filled in the strip mines and began to construct a golf course. Today, his Riverview Golf Course is one of the finest public golfing facilities in the Pittsburgh metropolitan area.

The purpose of the external analysis is to come up with an evaluation of the environment in which the firm operates. It should be an overall assessment, not simply a listing of favorable and unfavorable aspects. A firm in the computer industry might assess its environment as being volatile, subject to rapid technological change, increased miniaturization of components, and dominated by one large firm, IBM. Or a firm in the beer industry might assess its environment as being stable, growing very slowly, affected by economies of scale in production and distribution, and requiring heavy national advertising expenditures to build a brand name for an undifferentiated product.

B. Internal Evaluation

Look inside the organization to determine its strengths and weaknesses. In general, each functional area or characteristic of a firm may be evaluated as strong, neutral or weak. Following are six areas in which a firm may have pronounced strengths or weaknesses which should be considered when selecting a strategy for implementation.

1. *Finance.* Ratio analysis of the income statement and balance sheet will yield information on a firm's financial condition. A firm is usually in good financial condition if it can pay its bills (current ratio of 2:1, liquidity ratio of 1:1), has not borrowed too much money (long term debt to equity ratio less than 0.5), and earns money well (15% or greater average return on equity). Financial strength, including a top credit rating, will permit a firm to take advantage of new products or investment opportunities, or to repurchase its own shares.

■■■■■ A COMMENTARY on Reynolds Industries in the January 4, 1985 *Value Line Investment Survey* stated: "Over the course of the next three to five years, we project that [Reynolds'] annual cash flow will average some $1.3 billion plus . . . the excess cash is likely to be used for further share repurchases and/or a large acquisition. . . ."[4]

---

4. *Value Line* was right on target in its analysis. Later, in 1985, Reynolds acquired Nabisco, a leading food products company, and changed its name to RJR Nabisco. Then in 1988 the firm was taken private through a $25 billion leveraged buyout, by far the largest leveraged buyout ever as of this writing. In a leveraged buyout, an investor group borrows money to purchase the company, then repays the borrowed money from the firm's cash flow.

■■■■ IN THE 1950s Dow Chemical Company, under the leadership of Carl Gerstacker, rapidly expanded its capability to produce bulk chemicals. Its strong balance sheet and low interest rates (most Dow bonds issued in the 1950s had a coupon rate of 4% or less) gave Dow the opportunity to borrow heavily to expand capacity rapidly and establish itself as one of the world's largest chemical companies.

On the other hand, financial weakness may prevent a firm from taking advantage of attractive investment opportunities or investing in badly needed new plant and equipment.

2. *Management.* Some firms have unusual depth of management. One of the fine compliments often paid to General Electric is that if all its top executives should leave at once, the depth of its managers is so great that the corporation would continue to operate smoothly and efficiently. Indeed, in recent years, several top executives have gone from General Electric to head other major corporations, such as Larry Bossidy (Allied Signal), Stan Gault (Rubbermaid, Goodyear), and Tom Vander Slice (GTE, Apollo Computer). Andrew Carnegie knew the value of management well when he said, "Take away my factories, but leave my organization, and in four years I will have re-established myself."

3. *Brand name.* A well known brand name can be a great strength. See how many of the brand names left blank in the statements below come to mind as soon as you read them (look at the top of the next page for the missing word or words and the product's manufacturer):

Hold it together with _____ tape.

Get a cold drink from the _____ machine.

Wrap the meat in _____ _____ .

Put a _____ on the sore finger.

Take a picture with the _____ .

It's "_____ Time."

There's a _____ train under the Christmas tree.

_____ corn flakes.

Occasionally a brand name is literally too good, and it becomes the generic name for the product. This has happened with aspirin, cellophane, thermos and zipper, and came close with other products. For years, people would keep food cold in the "Frigidaire" (refrigerator) or make "Jello." For this reason, Xerox Corporation is very careful to emphasize that copies are made on the Xerox machine, not the other way around. Fiberglass is the generic name of the material made from finely spun glass. When spelled Fiberglas, it is also a registered trademark of the Dow-Corning Company.

Brand names can be a strong source of competitive advantage, particularly in the consumer products field. Many corporations employ marketing specialists whose job is to build brand identity for the firm's products, sometimes trying to make the customer perceive a difference in a product that is basically undifferentiated (aspirin, bananas, beer, flour, gasoline, salt, vodka). A Booz Allen & Hamilton study found that 19 of 24 leading consumer brands in 1923 were still the leading brands in 1983, and the others placed in the top five. No wonder makers of consumer products attach such importance to a good brand name.[5]

Some corporations may even change their name in an attempt to give the public a different (and presumably improved) image of their products. Thus National Cash Register changed its corporate name to the initials NCR in 1974 to downplay the importance of cash registers and launched an advertising campaign built around the theme, "NCR means computers." Hershey Chocolate Company changed its name to Hershey Foods in 1968 because, in the words of current Chairman Richard Zimmerman, "We think of ourselves as a manufacturer of food products, not just chocolate products."

One good way to see the history of brand names is to look through old issues of *Fortune* or *Time*. The products in many advertisements from the 1940s and 1950s will be familiar, but there will also be many brand names that have all but disappeared, such as Bell & Howell (home movie equipment) and Argus (35mm cameras).

4. *Market share.* Firms with large market share such as Anheuser-Busch (Budweiser beer), Coca-Cola, Eastman Kodak, General Motors, IBM, Kellogg, and Microsoft (computer software) have important advantages over firms in their industries with smaller market shares. High market share can permit a firm to take advantage of economies of

---

5. Paul B. Brown, ''New? Improved? The Brand-Name Mergers,''*Business Week*, October 21, 1985, pp. 108–110.

scale in manufacturing and national advertising campaigns.[6] With forty percent of the beer market, Anheuser-Busch can afford national advertising on prime time attractions such as sports championships in football or baseball. Coors, with less than ten percent of the beer market, does not have the financial resources to support frequent national advertising on prime time attractions.

5. *Location.* Real estate agents have long known the importance of location. So too location can be a major asset in most businesses, although its importance will vary with the type of business. Most service businesses (e.g., restaurants, motels, gas stations, drug stores, dry cleaners) are very conscious of the advantages of having a good location. That is why a bank in a medium sized city sought a location for a branch on the side of the road where outbound commuters would pass it, since they are more likely to transact business on the way home than on the way to work. (A Federal Reserve survey of financial service consumers showed that the convenience of a bank's location was the most important consideration of consumers, ahead even of the safety prospects for an investor's deposits.)

For some businesses, other factors may take precedence over location. Suppliers to large businesses (e.g., automobile parts to the automobile industry) may be able to offset higher shipping costs by locating in a state or county with lower labor costs or lower taxes, or both. Or national brewers may realize sufficient economies of scale by only brewing in a few large plants to offset higher shipping costs and permit effective price competition with smaller regional brewers who have very low shipping costs.

6. *Research and development.* Some firms spend large sums of money each year to develop new products. General Electric and Procter and Gamble are two firms that have long been known for their ability to develop and successfully market new products. At Hewlett-Packard, a leading maker of electronic test equipment and computers, two-thirds of its sales each year now come from products developed in the last five years. And at the Upjohn Company, a leading maker of pharmaceutical products, over ten percent of sales is spent each year to fund research and development projects, compared to an average of four percent for the Fortune 500 industrial firms as a whole. (Research and development will be considered further in Chapter 8.)

These are examples of areas that may be either weak or strong in a particular firm, and may thus have a major impact on the type of strategy

---

6. Market share is particularly important in mature consumer good markets, where demand for the product is not likely to increase much, if at all, from one year to the next. In such markets, any significant gain in market share must come at the expense of a competitor. Familiar examples of fierce competition for market share are rental cars (Hertz, Avis, National), shaving products (BIC and Gillette), breakfast foods (General Mills, Kellogg, Post), beer (Budweiser, Miller), and candy (Hershey, Mars, Nestle).

the firm can pursue. Other areas may be pertinent in particular industries, such as barrels of proven reserves for an oil company (Exxon), availability of engineers and skilled labor for an aerospace firm (Rockwell International), or an efficient distribution system for a large retailer (Wal-Mart). At Herman Miller, the maker of executive office furniture, good design has been a key skill for over fifty years. [7]

STEP II.
WHAT TRENDS DO WE SEE?

A firm should always be alert to trends that might affect it. A trend is an observable change in the course of events which could develop into a threat or an opportunity. Trends become apparent when a technological development or a better way of making a product or providing a service starts to gain acceptance. Most trends develop slowly over a period of years, thus providing sufficient lead time for identification and analysis. [8]

Television was one of the great growth industries of the decades following World War II. Yet primitive television systems were in use as early as 1907. Through use of a coding device called the Nipkow disc, a television picture the size of a postage stamp could be transmitted on standard a.m. radio waves. Improved systems with better resolution and a larger picture were in very limited use just prior to the outbreak of World War II, but the accelerated commercial development, including color, did not come until after World War II. [9]

Exhibit 3.2 gives examples of some well known inventions and innovations and the impact of their widespread acceptance and use. Note that none of these resulted in a product or service that was not previously available. What these inventions did was improve an existing product or provide a better service. Only rarely is a product so revolutionary that it creates an entirely new industry, as happened with the airplane (aviation) the radio transmitter and receiver (commercial broadcasting), or the computer (information processing). Consequently there is usually ample time to identify a trend when a major improvement is made in a product or service, such as replacing piston aircraft engines with jets, vacuum tubes with transistors (and later integrated circuits), or black

---

7. George Melloan, "Herman Miller's Secrets of Corporate Creativity," *The Wall Street Journal*, May 3, 1988, p. 23.

8. A trend should be distinguished from a fad, which may develop quickly but last only a short time. Hula hoops, pet rocks and Rubik's cubes are familiar examples of fads which had a brief moment of popularity. For a discussion of the difficulty of turning new technology into new products, see Peter F. Drucker, *Innovation and Entrepreneurship* (New York: Harper & Row, 1985), particularly Chapter 9, "Source: New Knowledge."

9. Peter Goldmark, *Maverick Inventor* (New York: Saturday Review Press/E.P. Dutton & Company, 1973). Chapters 2, 5, 6 and 7 summarize the invention and commercial development of television. Goldmark was also the inventor of the long playing record.

Invention	Commercial Availability	Impact
Zipper	1920s	Revolutionized garment industry. Hooks and eyes or buttons—the primary methods of fastening clothes together before the zipper—were clumsy, bulky and hard to use compared to the zipper.
Automobile	1920s	Caused rapid growth of many new businesses (fast food restaurants, gas stations, motels) and the largest road building program since the Roman Empire.
Nylon	1930s	A synthetic fabric that rapidly became a mainstay of the apparel industry due to its durability, ease of maintenance, low cost and ability to be dyed in almost any color or print.
Jet engine	1950s	Replaced piston driven engines in most commercial aircraft. Resulting increase in speed of travel led to the demise of ocean liners as the primary means to cross the Atlantic or Pacific oceans.
Long playing record	1950s	Improved quality, lowered cost and increased availability of music in the home. An entire Beethoven symphony or musical such as South Pacific or My Fair Lady could be put on a single disc.
Transistor	1950s	Replaced the vacuum tube in virtually all applications; made possible the high speed digital computer.
Air conditioning	1950s	Made office and factory work tolerable in the summer and contributed to the economic development of the South.
Xerography	1960s	Made inexpensive plain paper copying possible and virtually eliminated the need for carbon paper.
Personal computer	1980s	Replaced the typewriter as the basic word processing device.

Exhibit 3.2. Selected inventions and their impact.

and white television sets with color. Because most such improvements require years for implementation, an astute observer can often see major inventions or innovations progress as they gain widespread acceptance.

However, identifying a trend is not always adequate to insure that the evaluation of its impact will be at all correct. The first high speed digital computer designed for commercial use was marketed by Remington Rand in 1952 and called the Univac. Early estimates were that about 200 computers would be used outside government by the year 2,000. By 1990, there were over 70,000,000 computers in use in the United States alone and the number of new computers sold, including the increasingly popular microcomputers for home use, had reached 16,000,000 annually.

The computer industry's rapid growth is exemplified by the stories of Apple Computer and Compaq Computer. Founded in 1977 by 21 year old Steven Jobs, Apple's sales rose to $583 million in 1982, good enough for it to be ranked 411 on *Fortune*'s annual listing of the 500 largest industrial corporations. No other firm had attained a Fortune 500 ranking in such a short period of time. But Compaq Computer, founded in Dallas in 1983 by former corporate executives rather than an entrepreneur like Apple's Steve Jobs, surpassed Apple's record for growth, reaching a billion dollars in sales in just five years. By comparison, it took Apple seven years to reach a billion dollars in sales, but these are both extraordinary feats since virtually all growth in both firms was internally generated.

STEP III.
WHAT IS OUR BUSINESS?

This question asks for the firm's statement of corporate purpose or its mission statement, that is, what the corporation plans to do on an ongoing basis. Consider again the following mission statements from Chapter 2:

- The fire department. To save lives and protect property.
- A computer manufacturer. To meet the informational needs of its customers.

These mission statements are often just as useful for what they *do not* say as for what they *do* say. For both the fire department and the computer company, the customer's need is clearly identified (protection from fire, solving customer's informational needs), but the means of fulfilling that need are not. The mission of the fire department has not changed for centuries while ways to fight fires have. Similarly, the computer company's mission statement does not tie it to the computer as a way of satisfying customer needs, although most people naturally think of computers when a firm such as IBM or Apple is mentioned.

The Baldwin Locomotive Works provides a prime example of what too narrow a focus in the mission statement can do to a firm. For many years the dominant maker of steam locomotives for railroads at its mammoth Eddystone facility in Philadelphia, the Baldwin Locomotive Works went out of the locomotive business when it failed to see the threat of the diesel engine to the steam locomotive. While the total economics of diesel and steam power were similar, the diesel offered distinct advantages in many individual operating characteristics. It could start and stop with the press of a button, could go anywhere, was easy to drive, and, by regarding the units as building blocks, could be made up into a locomotive to suit a train of any size. Commercial production of diesel locomotives started in 1938, and by 1948 steam locomotive production had virtually stopped, as Exhibit 3-3 clearly shows. As if substantiating the trend, the cover of the March 1942 issue of *Fortune* showed a *diesel* engine at work in front of a large steel mill running at capacity.

The Electro-Motive Division of General Motors Corporation (originally a maker of gasoline-electric railcars which was acquired in 1930) became the world's largest maker of railroad engines. General Motors saw that powering a locomotive with a diesel engine was similar in technology to powering an automobile with a gasoline engine. Both diesel locomotives and automobiles used internal combustion engines and hence fit well with General Motors' implicit mission statement of making transportation equipment which uses internal combustion engines.

A good mission statement acts as a watershed for potential business activities. It gives guidance as to whether it makes sense for a firm to build a certain product or pursue a particular technology. Considerable thought may also be required to develop a mission statement that provides neither too much nor too little direction. Vague mission statements have little value. What does it mean when a firm states it will "be

Year	Steam locomotives	Diesel locomotives
1944*	326	750
1945*	115	800
1946	86	950
1947	69	1900
1948	86	2850
1949	57	1950
1950	12	2400

*World War II years

Exhibit 3.3. Locomotive orders, 1944–50, by type. Adapted from
J. B. Hollingsworth and P. B. Whitehouse, *American Railroads*
(London, England: Bison Books, 1977), p. 108.

a leader in developing innovative applications of proven technologies?" Since this statement could apply to many firms in many industries, it is of no help in determining what products or services a business should offer.

The mission statement may also change over time. ADT (American District Telegraph) started as a messenger service between businesses and established telegraph offices in major cities in the last part of the nineteenth century. When the invention of the telephone ended the need for the messenger service, ADT adapted its on-premises network of call boxes to fire and burglary monitoring services. ADT changed its mission from messenger service to on-premises protection, and it is now the largest firm in the security industry.

STEP IV.
WHAT ARE OUR STRATEGIC ALTERNATIVES?

Strategic alternatives refer to the broad based courses of action available to a firm to accomplish its mission statement. The set of strategic alternatives to be considered by each organization should be developed from a consideration of how the organization will interact with its environment. Firms in the same industry may follow quite different strategies, particularly if they are very different in size or market share.

■■■■■■■■ MONTGOMERY WARD and Sears Roebuck were close competitors as World War II drew to a close. Sewell Avery, head of Montgomery Ward, observed that there had always been a depression shortly after a war. His strategy for Ward's was as follows: wait for the depression he expected to come after World War II, then build new stores when land and labor were inexpensive, and be well positioned for the economic upturn he expected in about ten years. Sears, on the other hand, felt that there was large pent up demand from savings accrued during the war when consumer goods were scarce. Sears' strategy was to build new stores as soon as possible in the best locations it could purchase, paying top dollar if necessary, in order to be ready for the large increase it anticipated in post war consumer spending. Sears was right, and moved far out in front of Ward's as the nation's largest retailer.

■■■■■■■ FORD MOTOR COMPANY totally dominated the automobile market in the early 1920s. But Henry Ford, who had revolutionized the industry with his five dollar a day wage and the assembly line in 1913, did not change his strategy even though times had changed. He competed on price alone, eventually getting the price for the basic Model T down to

$300, and refused to offer optional equipment, different colors or financing to the customer. (Ford dealers would lose their dealership if they offered credit.) Meanwhile, under the direction of Alfred P. Sloan, Jr., General Motors offered more features, different colors and more highly styled cars at a price somewhat, but not a great deal, higher than Ford's Model T. It also offered financing for the prospective buyer through a new subsidiary, General Motors Acceptance Corporation. Sloan knew that the customer had progressed to wanting more than basic transportation. General Motors surpassed Ford in sales in 1929, and has never relinquished that lead.[10]

■■■■■■ XEROX acquired a promising young company called Scientific Data Systems (SDS) in 1969 in a transaction valued at almost one billion dollars as a way to enter the rapidly growing computer mainframe market. But in 1975, it wrote off the SDS acquisition as an $84 million loss, causing Xerox's first decrease in annual earnings per share growth for many years. Xerox was unable to make SDS competitive (or profitable) in a rapidly changing industry dominated by IBM. Had Xerox waited a few more years to make the acquisition, it would have seen both RCA and General Electric, two of the best known U.S. names in electronics, leave the computer industry. Xerox would also have had a better feel for the challenges it would face to become successful in the turbulent computer mainframe industry.

It is important to recognize what is and what is not a strategic alternative. An alternative is *strategic* if it relates to the way an organization goes about accomplishing its mission statement over the long run. Thus developing a new organizational structure, cutting costs or building a new plant are one-time actions that may be timely and important, but they are not strategic in the sense the word strategy is used in this book.

When formulating a set of strategic alternatives, the following should be kept in mind:

1. The organization can always keep doing what it has been doing. This is the *null* or *no change* alternative. Often this will be the preferred alternative, but in other cases failure to change may have a disastrous effect on the organization.
2. A second alternative that is usually possible is to *sell out*. This alternative should be recommended only as a last resort, because it is telling shareholders that someone else could do a better job of running

---

10. In the late 1980s, Ford actually had higher earnings than General Motors, although its total sales were only about two-thirds as much. Some feel that General Motors, like Henry Ford a half century earlier, had lost touch with the mainstream buyer of its automobiles.

the company than present management. However, if the price is high enough, this may be the best alternative. When corporate raider Boone Pickens indicated he would like to buy U.S. Steel (now USX) in 1985, U.S. Steel's chairman David Roderick said in effect, "Send a check for eight billion dollars and it's all yours." Pickens didn't respond.

3. **Keep the number of strategic alternatives small.** If the number of alternatives gets much above five, it is likely the mission statement is too broad, some of the alternatives are not really strategic in nature, or two or more of the alternatives are closely related and can be combined.

Occasionally, a strategic alternative will prove to be so successful that it causes the mission statement to be changed. For example, the BIC Pen Company started out in 1958 to be the leading firm in the low priced disposable ball point *pen* market. When BIC added low priced disposable lighters and shavers in the 1970s, it changed its mission statement to being the leading firm manufacturing disposable, inexpensive *consumer products*, a change that is clearly recognizable from reading BIC's annual reports. It also changed its name to BIC Corporation in recognition of its broadened product line.

STEP V:
SELECT THE BEST ALTERNATIVE FOR IMPLEMENTATION

The basic procedure in this step is to systematically weigh each strategic alternative against the mission statement and other relevant criteria. But what criteria are relevant? This is rarely an easy question to answer, since each individual may have a different idea of what is relevant. To some, the impact on earnings per share for the next few years may be the only important criterion. To others, maintaining a full line of service and products, even though some are marginally profitable, may be important. John Deere's primary source of sales and income is from heavy farm and industrial equipment. But Deere also makes a full line of farm tractors, lawnmowers, snowmobiles and snowblowers. Deere doesn't want a farmer who buys its tractors to have to go to another farm implement dealer for a snowblower or lawnmower where he might incidentally get interested in a competing line of farm equipment.

CRITERIA TO EVALUATE STRATEGIES

Four general criteria can be applied to any strategic alternative to see if it is a good fit with the mission statement and the firm's strengths and weaknesses.

1. Suitability

Will the strategic alternative actually accomplish what the firm wants accomplished? There may be a temptation to go too far afield in search of the right alternative; sometimes a closer look will show that the strategic alternative under consideration is not suitable in light of the mission statement.

2. Feasibility

Can the strategic alternative be implemented with the resources at hand, or if appropriate, have plans been made to obtain needed resources (e.g., increase long term debt if there is unused borrowing capacity)? This can also refer to the managerial talent available in the firm. If rapid expansion is contemplated, are there enough well trained individuals to fill the new management positions that will soon come into being?

3. Acceptability

Is the strategic alternative acceptable to all concerned? Here's where the values of managers may come into play. Howard Head's passionate dedication to the *metal* ski, which he invented, prevented him from seeing that synthetic materials such as fiberglass reinforced plastic would replace metal as the preferred material for making skis.

4. Risk

Is the degree of risk associated with the recommended strategy acceptable to the organization? Some degree of risk is inherent in every strategy, since no firm operates as a true monopoly with an assured demand. A decision not to change with the times can be just as risky as a decision to change too early, as the examples of Henry Ford, Sewell Avery, and the Baldwin Locomotive Works demonstrate.[11]

---

11. Risks and threats are often treated as if they were the same. However, there is an important difference. A *risk* by its nature affects everyone the same way. If it rains at a football game, players and spectators alike get rained on. A *threat* singles out one party with intention to harm or defeat that party. Thus a skilled quarterback on a football team may pose a threat to either run or pass the ball that the other team must counter if it is to win the game. For a further discussion of risks and threats, see Henry H. Beam and Thomas A. Carey, "The Risk-Threat Matrix: Key to Defensive Strategy," *Mid-American Journal of Business*, Fall 1991, pp. 39–44.

On the other hand, some of the greatest success stories in business have come from taking well calculated risks at a time when the firm was doing well.

■■■■■■ BY 1960 IBM was already the dominant factor in the computer business. But it spent $5 billion over the next four years to develop the first family of computers (the 360 series, representing all 360 degrees in a compass) which used the new integrated circuit technology. The 360 series was highly successful and solidified IBM's position of leadership in the field of computers. Even though development of the 360 series cost more than the World War II Manhattan project to build the atomic bomb, those associated with it felt the risks of doing nothing would have been much greater.[12]

Application of this five-step framework should bring to the fore enough information to permit the development of a comprehensive set of strategic alternatives. The strategic alternative selected for implementation depends on the resources available inside the firm, the opportunities available, the actions of competitors, and the values (including attitude toward risk) of those responsible for establishing the firm's strategy. While this discussion does not address implementation, keep in mind that implementation is fully as important to corporate success as the formulation of a good strategy.

It is also important to remember that there is no permanent solution to a business strategy problem. As time passes, a solution that once worked well may no longer be appropriate in light of changed internal or external conditions.

■■■■■■ FORMED IN 1946, Emery Air Freight became a highly successful air freight forwarder without incurring long term debt because it used commercial airlines to carry the packages. But in 1971 a new firm, Federal Express, was established which employed a new strategy to compete with Emery. Federal Express owned its own planes and flew all packages to a hub city (Memphis) each night where they were sorted and flown to their ultimate destination. Federal Express's strategy worked extremely well; by 1982 its revenues of $750 million were equal to those of Emery. Emery responded to this competitive threat by creating its own hub city (Dayton) and borrowing $130 million in 1981 to buy its own aircraft (giving it a hefty debt/equity ratio of 1.7:1) in an attempt to regain leadership in the industry it once dominated. External events in the form of a new competitor

12. T. A. Wise, "I.B.M.'s $5,000,000,000 Gamble," *Fortune Magazine*, September 1966, p. 113.

with a better strategy prompted a dramatic shift in the strategy Emery had employed so successfully for so many years. Then in April, 1989, Consolidated Freightways acquired Emery and merged it with its own air freight subsidiary, ending Emery's independent existence.[13]

Often the current strategy will be the preferred strategic alternative when the analysis is completed. That is why one of the strategic alternatives should always be the current strategy. But the importance of timing cannot be overemphasized. It may be disastrous to wait too long to change, as Henry Ford did by refusing to make anything but Model T's in any color but black. But changing too quickly can lead to equally disastrous results, as Xerox's ill-fated attempt to enter the computer mainframe business through the purchase of Scientific Data Systems in 1969 illustrates.

SUMMARY

Strategic planning is a demanding trade, part art and part science. The five step strategic planning framework discussed in this chapter should help make practicing that trade a little easier. It has the two characteristics that should be inherent in any sound strategic planning framework. First, it provides a way to bring order and purpose to what frequently appears at first to be a chaotic situation. Second, it suggests fundamental questions that should be asked about each strategic planning situation. While the answers may change with the situation, the questions themselves rarely change.

---

13. All air freight firms face an external threat to part of their business: the facsimile (or FAX) machine, which can deliver copies of printed matter over phone lines in minutes.

—4—

GROWTH AND DIVERSIFICATION

Growth (getting large) and diversification (going into different lines of business) are closely related concepts. Indeed, diversification, either through internal generation of new products or external acquisitions, is frequently used as a means to grow. Acquisitions may be made to enter new lines of business or to complement existing product lines.

All businesses start off by offering a single product or service, and some, such as oil companies and railroads, have historically grown and remained very large on the basis of that single product or service. A few present day manufacturing companies, such as Lincoln Electric of Cleveland, the world's leading maker of welding equipment and supplies, have grown and prospered for decades as single product firms. However, today virtually all large businesses (e.g., the Fortune 500 companies) are diversified to some extent, and a Lincoln Electric is clearly the exception rather than the rule.

REASONS TO BECOME LARGER

Here are four reasons why a business might want to become larger:

1. Maximize Total Profits

This classical economic reason, if taken literally, means that new products should be developed or new firms acquired as long as there is a net addition to profits. This decision rule may be represented graphically as shown in Exhibit 4.1, where potential acquisition alternatives are rank ordered according to their total profit, and nothing else. Acquisition alternatives one through four would add to total profits and hence, according to this decision rule, should be made. On the other

41

hand, acquisition alternatives five and six would not be made since they would entail a loss, thereby reducing total profitability.

While this criterion has the advantage of being easy to apply, most managers would want to consider more factors than total profits alone, such as the future attractiveness of the acquired firm's products, the fit between the two firm's product lines, additional financial requirements, return on investment or cash flow.

2. Get Large Per Se

To many executives, size is important in and of itself irrespective of such considerations as return on investment. Top executives of the largest Fortune 500 companies such as Exxon, General Motors, and General Electric not only receive the largest salaries (amounts in excess of $1,000,000 are becoming commonplace for top executives of such firms), but also have the most status in terms of being spokesman for the corporate world.[1] Continued growth, no matter how attained, has long been viewed favorably in our Western society.

3. Take Advantage of Economies of Scale

In many capital intensive industries, there are obvious advantages associated with economies of scale. Steel mills, automobile assembly plants and breweries are familiar examples of large facilities designed to produce large quantities of a standardized output at the lowest cost possible.

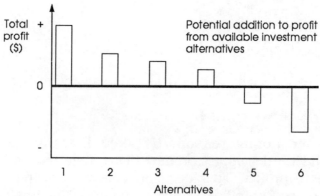

Exhibit 4.1. Acquisition alternatives ranked by total profit.

1. For example, see J. Byrnes, "The Flap Over Executive Pay: Investors, Employees and Academics Are Asking, How Much Is Enough?" *Business Week*, May 6, 1991, pp. 90–96, and Graef S. Crystal, "Why CEO Compensation Is So High," *California Management Review*, Fall 1991, pp. 9–29.

4. Dominate a Market

It takes a large firm to dominate a large market, such as Exxon in oil, USX (formerly U.S. Steel) in steel, General Motors in automobiles or IBM in computers. Such firms are often the price leaders in the markets they serve. They can also afford to advertise nationally and to supply regional markets from regional plants. Large firms can also afford to hire good people, train them well, and offer attractive compensation packages to retain them. Because of such advantages, firms may deliberately try to grow large to gain or keep a dominant position in their major markets.

The ultimate in size would be to have a monopoly, as John D. Rockefeller nearly attained in the 1890s in oil, controlling an estimated 75% of the U.S. market. In 1911, his Standard Oil Company was broken up into 34 separate companies (today's Exxon is the direct descendent of the original firm) to foster competition.[2]

All four of these reasons assume that size per se is desirable. However, they make little attempt to justify getting bigger in terms of financial measures of performance such as return on equity or return on sales. Nor do they explicitly seek to help a business adapt and survive. They implicitly assume a static world, and hence are poor guides for making strategic decisions in today's often turbulent business environment. Nevertheless, getting bigger has an enduring appeal in terms of human nature, which associates size with status and power.

REASONS TO DIVERSIFY

We will now consider the two primary reasons a business might want to diversify, recognizing that in the process a likely side effect will also be to get larger.

1. To Survive

Many management writers, including Peter Drucker, argue that the primary task of a business (or any organization) is survival. Since no product lasts forever, diversification is seen as a way to survive. It is not uncommon in many firms for half or more of their sales to come from products they did not make five or ten years earlier. Consider the example of U.S. Steel, the

---

2. The country's first billionaire, Rockefeller was generous with his money even if he was ruthless in the way he obtained it. By the time of his death in 1937 at the age of 98, he had given over $500,000,000 to support public causes, including $35,000,000 from 1890–1910 to establish the University of Chicago. Americans were inherently suspicious of monopolies, and they were made illegal by the Sherman Antitrust Act of 1890.

country's largest firm upon its formation at the turn of the century with over a billion dollars of assets and still its largest steel producer. In 1982, it acquired Marathon Oil as a way to diversify out of the steel business, which had been on a steady decline in the United States since the 1960s. In 1984, slightly over half of U.S. Steel's revenues and over eighty percent of its operating profits came from oil and gas; steel operations were marginally profitable after showing multi-million dollar losses in 1982 and 1983.[3]

From 1850–1875, the Wells Fargo Company was one of the country's best known institutions, moving mail, money (often in the form of gold) and people by stagecoach all across the West. When the railroads expanded across the continental United States in the last quarter of the nineteenth century, the demand for stagecoach services fell rapidly. Wells Fargo then changed its primary business from operating stagecoaches to being a bank, an ancillary service initially offered for the convenience of its stagecoach passengers. Today, Wells Fargo is a well known San Francisco bank, and the once famous Wells Fargo stagecoaches exist only in western movies and museums.

2. To Minimize Risk

The assumption here is that business risk can be precisely defined and quantified, and that mathematical techniques can be employed to minimize it.[4] This approach may be used both to increase chances for survival and to provide guidelines for acquisitions. While acquiring a firm in the same or a similar business should not reduce risk, acquiring one in an unrelated business should reduce it.[5] The rationale is that when one division is down (original equipment auto parts), another division (aerospace) may be up, and so on for all divisions. As a result year-to-year earnings fluctuations should be less than what they would have been with only a single product or closely related product lines.

Here is an excellent summary of this way of thinking:

> In a year marked by substantial economic uncertainty for many industrial companies, Rexnord's operating performance demonstrates the underlying strengths of the company. Rexnord is broadly diversified in both the products it manufactures and the markets it serves. More than half of the 1981 volume came from replacement parts and nearly

---

3. U.S. Steel 1984 Annual Report. In 1986 it also acquired Texas Oil & Gas and changed its name to USX Corporation.

4. For example, see David B. Hertz, *New Power for Management* (New York: McGraw-Hill, 1969).

5. Note that diversification will not eliminate what is sometimes called *systematic risk*: the risk that a certain event or events (energy shortage, natural disaster, inflation) will affect all aspects of a business about equally. Sometimes it is possible to obtain insurance against certain types of risks, such as natural disasters.

one-third of our business from international markets. Thus, we are not dependent on any single market, product, or country for our economic growth. This planned diversification has helped to offset the declines experienced by many of the company's capital goods markets this year.
Source: 1981 Rexnord Annual Report

Very sophisticated techniques have been developed to measure risk and assess corporate performance under a range of economic conditions. There are two shortcomings to these techniques. First, the mathematical techniques (e.g., regression analysis) are much more precise than the quality of the input data. Second, and probably more important, few executives really believe that the worst case assumptions for each major line of business could ever occur at the same time. In short, almost all executives have a natural tendency to view the future in an optimistic way. (The author has yet to read a Chairman's letter in an Annual Report that wasn't optimistic about the company's future, no matter how bleak current operations appeared.)

Starting in the mid-1960s, some top managers questioned the desirability of growth or diversification, or both. In 1970 General Electric, often at the forefront in management innovations, reviewed its financial performance for the decade of the 1960s. It found that sales had increased steadily, but that earnings per share growth had not kept pace while return on equity had steadily declined. Terming this "profitless growth," General Electric sought to remedy the deterioration of its financial performance through a new corporate planning system.

General Electric explicitly recognized that sales growth per se is not enough to insure a high level of financial performance. Recall that according to the first reason to grow, to maximize total profits, acquisitions would be made and new products developed as long as they added to total profitability. However, an acquisition that requires extensive corporate assets to provide a small return, less, for example, than could be attained from government securities, is not a good investment.

A more reasonable set of decision rules might include a requirement that each new acquisition or new product have a minimum market share, return on equity or return on assets by a certain time. Consequently some acquisitions that would add to size or to total profits might be excluded according to these more rigorous criteria. These criteria lead to the view that a diversified firm's set of products or businesses should be considered as a *portfolio* where each member of the portfolio has to meet specific investment criteria.

Methods for evaluating the performance of a product or potential investment, including discounted cash flow and internal rate of return, have been well developed in the field of finance. But these methods only provide information. It remains the responsibility of the general manager to use this information together with other pertinent criteria (legal, political, environmental), including his or her personal experience, to make wise decisions for the firm.

██████████ IN 1967, North American Aviation, a major west coast aerospace firm, and Rockwell Standard, a Pittsburgh based automotive supplier, merged to form the company that we know today as Rockwell International. The idea was to apply North American's advanced technology to automotive products and Rockwell's manufacturing expertise to aerospace production. Additionally it was hoped that the aerospace and automotive businesses, both naturally cyclical in nature, would not both have bad years at the same time. The results have been excellent. Today Rockwell is both a leading automotive parts supplier and a major defense contractor (the B1 bomber and the space shuttle) which boasts a return on equity of nearly twenty percent and earnings per share that have increased steadily since 1975. The following, taken from the Rockwell International 1985 Second Quarter Report, states the company's mission well:

Rockwell International Corporation is a major multi-industry company applying advanced technology to a wide range of products in its automotive, aerospace, electronics and general industries businesses.

Rockwell's 1985 acquisition of Allen-Bradley Company, long a privately held, Milwaukee based maker of high quality electric control systems, fits well with this mission statement.

HOW MUCH DIVERSIFICATION?

Some degree of diversification is probably desirable for most firms, but too much, or totally unrelated, diversification often causes difficulties.[6] One of the major problems is that by definition diversification means going into new businesses, and this requires the ability to manage these new businesses. This is not always an easy task to accomplish. For example, Exxon, the world's largest oil company, knows a great deal about

---

6. Geraldine Brooks, "Some Firms Find that the Push to Diversify Was a Costly Mistake," *The Wall Street Journal*, October 2, 1984, p. 33.

finding, refining and marketing oil. But it made multi-million dollar mistakes that only a firm of its size could absorb without difficulty when it tried to develop its own line of office products in the 1970s and when it acquired Reliance Electric, a maker of electric motors, in 1974. (When it acquired Reliance, Exxon thought it was buying technology to make a more efficient electric motor at a time when energy prices were rising. Not only did the motor not work as promised, but energy prices started to fall not long after.)

A few firms have managed to diversify unusually well. Raytheon, 3M, and Sara Lee (formerly Consolidated Foods) are three firms which have reported increased earnings per share almost every year for the past decade and each has a return on equity that is consistently above fifteen percent. But there is still some commonality in the products of these firms. Raytheon's businesses are all based on technology (missiles, electronics, major household appliances); almost all of 3M's more than 6,000 products relate to applying coatings to surfaces; and Sara Lee makes consumer products that are sold through the same distribution channels (Sara Lee frozen foods, Hanes knitwear and hosiery).

Even if a firm is reasonably successful in diversifying, it may have a difficult time convincing the investing public of its success. Diversified firms usually sell for a discount over what the value of the separate businesses would be worth if price/earnings multiples were assigned to each product group. The reason for this is that there is little, if anything, that a firm can do in terms of diversification that an individual investor can't do in terms of his or her own portfolio of investments. For years, R.J. Reynolds was the nation's leading tobacco firm, and highly profitable as well. Investors perceived Reynolds as a packaged goods company, and didn't understand its moves into shipping (Sea-Land, which pioneered the containerized cargo ship) and energy (Aminoil). In 1983, Reynolds divested itself of Sea-Land by declaring a special dividend of Sea-Land stock to its shareholders, and in 1984 it sold Aminoil to Phillips Petroleum.

Then in 1985 it merged with Nabisco Brands, a leading producer of consumer goods, primarily food products, a diversification move which was perceived as fitting very well with Reynolds' image as a packaged foods company. It also changed its name to RJR Nabisco. In one of the sensational corporate news stories of 1988, RJR Nabisco was taken private through a leveraged buyout for 25 billion dollars, the largest in history. Some market analysts felt that the acquisition of Nabisco Brands did not work out as well as planned, and that the firm was worth considerably more than its stock was selling for if it was split into pieces and sold.[7]

SUMMARY

There isn't a single answer to the question, "how much diversification is enough?" Firms that don't diversify soon enough (Baldwin Locomotive Works) may not survive, but firms that diversify too much, or in the wrong areas (Exxon), may hamper their own growth and profitability. The strategic planning process should consider diversification as an alternative, and not as an end in itself. The next two chapters discuss the process of strategy formulation in the diversified firm.

---

7. For a lively account of the takeover battle, see Bryan Burrough and John Helyer, *Barbarians at the Gate* (New York: Harper Collins, 1990).

—5—

STRATEGY FORMULATION IN THE DIVERSIFIED FIRM

The procedure for solving business strategy problems discussed in Chapter 3 was designed for firms which produced a single product or a series of related products. Indeed, through the first half of this century, almost all large firms were one product or related product firms. Exhibit 5.1 lists the ten largest U.S. industrial corporations in 1909 ranked by assets. (The inside back cover of this book lists the ten largest U.S. industrial companies in 1991 ranked by sales. Before looking at it, try making out your own list of the top ten firms. Only one firm is on both lists: the original Standard Oil Company, which is now called Exxon.) The nation's ten largest retailing firms are listed on the page facing the inside back cover.

Well into this century a firm's name was often synonymous with the product it produced (Ford Motor Company, Swift Meatpacking, U.S. Steel, American Tobacco, Eastman Kodak).[1] However, as indicated in Chapter 4, there are reasons why even the most successful one product or related product firms should consider diversifying. To many executives, the question is not whether to diversify, but to what extent, in what way, and when.

During World War II the advances in military technology (computers, jet engines, nuclear power, radar) provided natural opportunities for one product or related product firms to diversify. After the war, television, computers and aerospace replaced steel, railroads and automobiles as the great growth industries. Firms no longer necessarily made products for a single industry. During the decade of the 1960s, diversification became the rule rather than the exception. Many firms diversified by acquiring other firms with similar products (Coca-Cola acquiring Minute Maid orange juice in 1966; PepsiCo acquiring Pizza Hut in 1977 and

---

1. Frequently the firm was named after its founder, e.g., Henry Ford, H. J. Heinz, George Eastman and Andrew Carnegie (Carnegie Steel Company, the forerunner of U.S. Steel).

Rank	Corporation	Total assets (millions)	Primary Product
1	U.S. Steel Corp.	$ 1,822.0	Steel
2	Standard Oil Company	371.7	Oil
3	American Tobacco Co.	286.0	Tobacco
4	International Mercantile Marine Company	202.5	Shipping
5	International Harvester	172.8	Farm equipment
6	Amalgamated Copper Co.	170.2	Copper
7	Central Leather Co.	138.3	Leather goods
8	Pullman Company	130.6	Railroad cars
9	Armour & Company	124.8	Meat packing
10	American Sugar Refining	124.3	Sugar

Exhibit 5.1. Ten largest U.S. industrial corporations in 1909, ranked by assets. Adapted from A.D.H. Kaplan, *Big Enterprise in a Competitive System* (Washington, D.C.: The Brookings Institution, 1954), p. 145.

Kentucky Fried Chicken in 1986). But the real change occurred when an increasing number of firms acquired other firms whose products had no logical relation to each other. The first to do this successfully was Textron under the guidance of its founder, Royal Little.[2] Little's aim was to free Textron of the dependence it had on the highly cyclical and marginally profitable New England textile industry. Today Textron's major business divisions are aerospace (Bell Helicopters), consumer products (Talon zippers, Homelite chain saws) and industrial products (automobile parts, machine tools). As a point of interest, Textron has not been directly involved in the textile industry since 1964.

THE DEVELOPMENT OF CONGLOMERATES

Many firms followed Textron's example during the 1960s. A rising stock market and high price/earnings ratios greatly facilitated the financing of

2. Although few people know about him today, Royal Little (1896–1989) was one of the best known businessmen of his generation. For a description of the founding of Textron and the subsequent changes that made Textron the first conglomerate, see his highly entertaining book *How to Lose $100,000,000 and Other Valuable Advice* (Boston, MA: Little, Brown and Company, 1979). Don't be misled by the title; he actually made many times the amount he claims he lost.

acquisitions through exchange of stock. These firms soon became known as "conglomerates."[3] Financial considerations became the primary criteria for operating the firm. Management's goal was to produce a steady increase in earnings per share each year. It sought to minimize fluctuations in earnings per share by broad diversification and by strong centralized financial controls. Some well known industrial firms frequently classified as conglomerates are given in Exhibit 5.2, together with their Fortune 500 rank in 1990.

Regardless of the way they diversified, these firms present a more difficult problem in terms of solving problems of business strategy. The five step framework developed in Chapter 3 needs to be modified as shown in Exhibit 5.3 to accommodate to the diversity inherent in these firms. The major modifications are in the steps concerning the mission statement (Step III) and the selection of the best strategic alternative for implementation (Step V). Both these modifications serve to bring financial considerations to the fore, such as return on investment, cash flow or payback period. Beyond dollars, it is difficult to find meaningful common criteria to compare and evaluate the attractiveness of distinctly different businesses.[4]

Fortune 500 Rank	1991 Sales (millions)	Firm Name	Primary Products
5	$ 60,236	General Electric	Electrical equipment, home appliances, broadcasting, leasing
16	21,262	United Technologies	Jet engines, industrial products, defense
36	11,882	Allied-Signal	Chemicals, auto parts, electronics
62	7,913	TRW	Auto parts, spacecraft, financial services
63	7,840	Textron	Aerospace, power tools, auto parts
87	6,117	LTV	Steel, aerospace, energy

Exhibit 5.2. Conglomerates in the top 100 of the Fortune 500 industrial firms, 1991. Adapted from *Fortune Magazine*, April 20, 1992, pp. 220–239.

3. For a description of the first conglomerate corporations, see John Brooks, *The Go-go Years* (New York: Weybright and Talley, 1973). No one seems to know the origin of the word conglomerate, but it came into common usage in the 1960s.

4. Market share is sometimes used as a criterion to compare businesses. However, it is not easy to precisely or meaningfully define most markets. For example, does Mercedes-Benz have a small share of the total automobile market or does it have the dominant share of the luxury car market?

Step	Modification
I. Where are we now?	Done for each major division.
II. What trends do we see?	Done for each major division.
III. What is our mission statement?	Often stated in broad based financial terms for the entire corporation (a meta-mission statement). Units or divisions may have their own mission statements.
IV. What are our strategic alternatives?	Stated for each major division.
V. Select the best strategic alternative.	Done for each major division, then the best division alternatives are combined to form the overall corporate plan.

Exhibit 5.3. Modifications for diversified firms.

MODIFYING THE MISSION STATEMENT

The result is that the mission statement of a conglomerate of necessity takes the form of a "meta-mission statement," such as to have a return on equity in excess of fifteen percent or to maximize shareholder wealth. Exhibit 5.4 gives a summary of the mission statement and performance objectives of Textron Corporation. Note how frequently specific numbers relating to financial performance are mentioned. (This example is quite unusual, since corporations are rarely so explicit in stating their goals publicly.) In contrast, the mission statement of a single product firm is directly related to the nature of the product produced or service provided. The conglomerate or broadly diversified firm should also have a set of mission statements, one for each major product line, in addition to the financially oriented meta-mission statement.

The difficulties in formulating mission statements for conglomerate firms are as follows:

1. The meta-mission statement has little meaning because it is so broad-based. It is akin to saying the purpose of a business is to survive or to maximize profit.
2. The need to allocate scarce resources (money, materials, management) between diverse products usually leads to development of a central planning group to oversee the separate divisions and make these resource allocations.
3. The allocation of resources is often done according to financial criteria alone since dollars are the only commonly accepted measure

The Textron Concept and Objectives

Textron is founded on the principle of balanced diversification, designed on the one hand to afford protection against economic cycles and product obsolescence and on the other to provide a means for participating in new markets and new technologies. The key elements are balance and flexibility in a rapidly changing world.

Textron seeks to be distinctive in its products and services — distinctive as to technology, design, service and value. Superior performance will be achieved by way of excellence and quality.

Textron operations are conducted through a number of Divisions in five Groups — Aerospace, Consumer, Industrial, Metal Product and Creative Capital. Each Division carries on its business under its own name and with its own organization. Textron's management philosophy is based on decentralization of day-to-day operations, coupled with centralized coordination and control to assure overall standards and performance.

There are three priorities: People development. Internal profit growth. New initiatives.

During the recent recession and the current slow recovery, added emphasis has been placed on internal growth and refinement of operations.

In 1972 Textron set objectives for the ten-year period from 1972 to 1982. The specific targets for average annual compound rates of growth are:

Sales: 8%, to $3.5 billion in 1982.
Progress, 1972 to date: 14%, to $2.5 billion in 1975.

Net income: 10%, to $200 million in 1982.
Progress, 1972 to date: 5%, to $96 million in 1975.

Earnings per share: 10%, to $6.00 in 1982.
Progress, 1972 to date: 4%, to $2.58 in 1975.

Exhibit 5.4. Textron Corporation Concept and Objectives as of 1975. (Reprinted with permission of Textron Inc.)

of performance between divisions making very different products. Suboptimal decisions can easily occur since any unique non-financial needs (special production processes, local availability of skilled labor) are not likely to be taken into account by the financially oriented members of top management.

4. Outsiders (investors, customers, bankers) have a difficult time knowing exactly what the firm does.

SUMMARY

The conglomerate represents diversification taken to the extreme. Nevertheless, most large firms will continue to feel the need to seek some degree of diversification to protect themselves against the threat of having all their eggs in one basket. And the more they diversify, the more they will have to deal with the sorts of difficulties conglomerates have to face.

Since the mid-1960s, there has been great interest in developing techniques to deal with resource allocation and strategic planning in diversified firms. We will discuss what general managers need to know about them in Chapter 6.

6

PORTFOLIO PLANNING MODELS

Diversified firms require more planning than one product or related product firms. Portfolio planning models, the basic approach to strategy formulation in such firms, assume that there is a group at corporate headquarters charged with overall strategic planning. This group decides (or recommends) which products should be emphasized, which acquisitions should be pursued, and which products should be dropped or sold. There is much more flexibility here than in planning for a single product firm. (There is also more overhead, since a one product firm usually requires a smaller staff.) The planner in a diversified firm is like the owner of a professional sports team who can make trades to improve the team during the season. The planner in a single product firm is like the college coach who has to go through the season with the talent enrolled at the start of the year.

This chapter reviews two popular approaches to portfolio planning developed during the 1960s and 1970s, the Boston Consulting Group approach and the McKinsey/General Electric approach. Both are still widely used, although not with the zeal they were a decade ago. They are often modified or blended together to suit the needs of a particular firm or industry.

THE BOSTON CONSULTING GROUP APPROACH

In the 1960s, the Boston Consulting Group made a major contribution to strategic planning in diversified firms. This contribution was to consider the attributes of each business or product, as appropriate, according to its potential for growth and present market share in the form of a growth/share matrix. The wide use of the BCG growth/share matrix is due to its simplicity and its intuitive appeal, characteristics which managers readily appreciate.

The growth/share matrix is based on the assumption that cash flow is a measure of success and is related to two dimensions: the *market share* and the *market growth rate* of the business or product. These dimensions in turn are related to cash use and cash generation as follows:

1. *Cash use* is a function of the growth rate of the market. A fast growing market requires increased investment to maintain the product's position in the market.
2. *Cash generation* is a function of the market share of the product. High market share implies manufacturing efficiencies which should result in high profit margins per unit sold. High margins plus high volume should lead to high cash generation.

A firm's products or businesses can be classified according to their relative market share and market growth and plotted on a two by two matrix which shows net cash flows as shown in Exhibit 6.1. According to the BCG approach, there is a preferred strategy for products or businesses in each quadrant.

Quadrant I: Future Stars, Problem Children, or ?'s

These are low market share and high market growth products. Products and businesses in this category generate little cash due to low market share, but require large amounts of cash to survive due to the high growth rate of the business. The preferred strategy is, therefore, either a drive for leadership (toward a high market share position) or a liquidation of the existing position.

Quadrant II: Stars

Stars are high market share and high growth products. Stars, through their high market share, generate a substantial amount of cash which is largely used up by the need to maintain their position in a market with a high rate of growth. Star products and businesses represent the future of the company and hence, according to the BCG approach, call for an aggressive marketing strategy to increase or hold market share. As growth slows, the stars will start throwing off cash, becoming "cash cows."

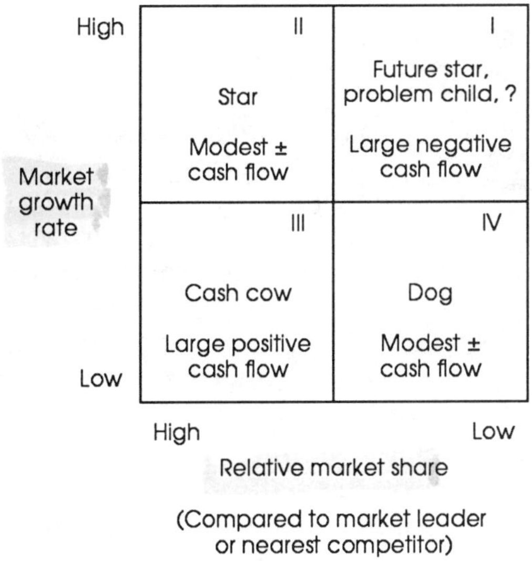

High

	II	I
	Star	Future star, problem child, ?
	Modest ± cash flow	Large negative cash flow

Market growth rate

	III	IV
	Cash cow	Dog
	Large positive cash flow	Modest ± cash flow

Low

High   Low

Relative market share

(Compared to market leader or nearest competitor)

Exhibit 6.1. BCG growth/share multi-business planning matrix.

Quadrant III: Cash Cows

Cash cows are high market share and low market growth products. These products and businesses, due to their high market share and the benefit of the experience curve in both manufacturing and marketing, generate more cash than is required by the low growth markets in which they operate. Cash cow products provide the main source of cash and earnings to the firm. The preferred strategy with cash cows, according to BCG logic, is to use them to generate cash and avoid share building strategies which tend to be too expensive given the already high market share and slow market growth. (In the mature beer and soft drink markets, a gain in market share of *one* percent is considered significant and difficult to attain.) Hence the primary objective of these products is the generation of short term profits to finance long term corporate development programs.

Quadrant IV: Dogs

Dogs are low market share and low market growth products. Products in this category generate little cash, but they don't require much cash, either. Dogs include unsuccessful new brands and mature products with declining sales. The preferred strategy in this category is to maximize cash generation even if this leads to product or business liquidation.

Given that firms might find themselves with products or businesses in all four categories, the portfolio concept requires a balance of products and supporting relationships among the various products. A balanced approach would call for the transfer of cash from cash cows to problem children, while the product or business flow is from problem children to stars and from stars to cash cows. These planned changes in a portfolio over time are based on the premise that high growth products require cash, while low growth products should provide cash. The overall product portfolio should be balanced, avoiding a situation where a portfolio has too many problem children (which require considerable amounts of cash) or too many cash cows (which generate cash but are subject to low or possibly even negative growth).

The BCG framework, in its simplest and most common form, does not explicitly take into account the nature of the individual products, the projected and desired performance of the various products, or the risk and cost of operation. Some companies modify the BCG framework to incorporate profitability and forecasts of the future performance of the various products.

DIFFICULTIES WITH THE APPROACH

At first glance, the BCG growth/share matrix seems to offer guidance to manage any portfolio of businesses. In practice, matters are not that simple. Here are eight commonly encountered problems that cause difficulties for the model:

1. The choice of measures for market share or for market growth are not always easy to make. Is Dr Pepper, a specialty non-cola soft drink, a small factor in the soft drink business, as it would be if measured against the industry leader, Coca-Cola?[1] Or is it the dominant firm when measured against the specialty non-cola soft drinks, such as Coca-Cola's Mr. Pibb? Further, is Dr Pepper part of the low growth soft drink industry or is it part of the high growth specialty soft drink market?

   Choice of measures could place Dr Pepper in any of the four categories, as shown in Exhibit 6.2. A framework of analysis should provide consistent and unambiguous results regardless of the choice of data, and this is rarely easy to do with the BCG matrix.

---

1. The correct spelling is without a period: Dr Pepper.

Dr Pepper's Market Share Compared to:		Industry Growth Measured Against:		BCG Category
Coca-Cola[a]	Low	All soft drinks	Low	Dog
Itself[b]	High	All soft drinks	Low	Cash cow
Coca-Cola[a]	Low	Specialty soft drinks	High	Future star
Itself[b]	High	Specialty soft drinks	High	Star

a Coca-Cola is the market leader for *all* soft drinks
b Dr Pepper is the market leader for *specialty* soft drinks

Exhibit 6.2. Four BCG categorizations for Dr Pepper using different measures for market share and market growth.

2. The BCG matrix is not derived from empirical (real world) data. It is based on assumptions which yield a logically consistent model. However, simply because a model is logically consistent when presented using chalk and a blackboard does not mean that it is a good representation of reality. Thus there is no assurance that applying the BCG matrix to a particular firm will provide the desired strategic results.

3. It places a premium on financial skill rather than on an understanding of how to run the businesses that happen to be in a portfolio. Short term results may be stressed at the expense of long range opportunities.

4. The model gives useful guidance for dealing with businesses that are clearly promising or clearly failing (divest, harvest), but it is much less helpful when dealing with the vast majority of businesses that are about average (near the center of the matrix). It also needs to be applied cautiously to businesses that are cyclical, but over the long run may be highly profitable (farm machinery, automobiles). It would be a mistake to cut back or divest in a downturn if the cycle turns up shortly thereafter.

5. The concept does not explicitly account for product groupings built on a common technology, rather than specific products. For example, at Texas Instruments the digital products segment at one time included mini-computers, data terminals, calculators and watches.

6. Shared costs are not considered. Assume products A, B and C each use a common component (electric motors, gasoline engines) that can be made or purchased for lower unit costs as volume increases. If product A is a star, B is a cash cow and C a dog, the model does

not explicitly consider the impact on the cost of A if B or C, or both, are discontinued.

7. The matrix approach does not consider the potential advantages of vertical integration (e.g., capturing profits at each stage of manufacture, assuring a source of supply). Each product or segment is considered a separate entity which stands on its own merits independent of the firm's other products.

8. Administrative difficulties may arise. How do you get good managers to work for businesses that have been identified as dogs and are likely to be sold? Such a classification can become a self-fulfilling prophecy: poor business, poor managers, poor results and eventual sale or divestiture.

These shortcomings have considerably reduced the appeal of the BCG matrix approach to strategic planning for many firms. Nevertheless the BCG approach does provide useful insights into the nature of strategic planning. It is particularly useful when a firm is considering the acquisition of another firm or the divestiture of one or more of its own divisions.[2]

THE STRATEGIC BUSINESS UNIT APPROACH

Like the Boston Consulting Group growth/share matrix, the Strategic Business Unit approach has become a standard way of planning for many large diversified corporations. The Strategic Business Unit (SBU) approach to planning was developed in the 1970s by General Electric (GE) with the help of the management consulting firm of McKinsey & Company.[3] It uses the same basic concepts as the four cell matrix of the Boston Consulting Group, but there are important differences.

The BCG matrix was developed on the basis of logic, and then sold primarily on the basis of its intuitive appeal rather than on the results obtained using it. In contrast, General Electric's impetus to improve its performance came from inside the firm itself. It wanted to reverse the "profitless growth" it had experienced during the decade of the 1960s

2. The approach is described in a number of pamphlets in the Boston Consulting Group's "Perspectives" series written by Bruce D. Henderson, the firm's founder. For a critical review of the approach, see George S. Day, "Diagnosing the Product Portfolio," *Journal of Marketing*, April 1977, pp. 29–38. Also see Walter Kichel III, "Oh Where, Oh Where Has My Little Dog Gone? Or My Cash Cow? Or My Star," *Fortune*, November 2, 1981, pp. 148–154.

3. Much of the historical information on strategic business units given here comes from the General Electric Company publication (circa 1977) *Strategic Management at General Electric*. See also William K. Hall, "SBUs: Hot, New Topic in the Management of Diversification," *Business Horizons*, February 1978, pp. 17–25; and Walter Kichel III, "Playing by the Rules of the Corporate Strategy Game," *Fortune*, September 24, 1979, p. 110.

when growth in earnings per share did not keep pace with sales growth and return on equity declined.

A review of General Electric's broad array of products showed that it was competing with 70 of the largest 200 manufacturing firms in the United States. This lent credence to its claim of being the most diversified company in the world.

To deal effectively with this diversity, GE devised separate organizational structures for control and planning:

- the structure for *control* continued to be the traditional organization chart with line and staff responsibilities clearly delineated.
- the structure for *planning* consisted of grouping products or product groups according to the competition faced.

This entailed rearrangement of the traditional organization chart *for planning purposes only*.

The building block of this planning system is called a Strategic Business Unit, or, in abbreviated form, simply "SBU." An SBU is defined as:

- a unit whose manager has complete responsibility for integrating all functions into a strategy against identifiable external competitors.

Some examples of SBUs are given in Exhibit 6.3. Note that a company that has only *one* product will have only *one* SBU. This emphasizes that the SBU concept is primarily intended for use by diversified firms.[4]

The Business Screen

In its original form, the head of each SBU is expected to go through a rigorous product review process each year. The purpose of this product review process is to bring to the corporate level a set of strategic plans, one for each SBU, which can be reviewed for resource allocation. The evaluation of the attractiveness of an SBU for further resource allocation is done through use of a device called the "business screen," which has two dimensions: *business strength* and *industry attractiveness*. The phrase "multi-factor assessment" means that many factors were taken into account in assessing both the business strength and industry

---

4. A predecessor to the SBU concept was the product (or brand) manager approach developed and used by both consumer goods and manufacturing companies. A product manager is usually in charge of one or more product programs, which are really strategic plans for serving a particular market segment, including product design, distribution channels, advertising, promotion, selling and customer service. For a further discussion see *The Product Manager System, Experiences in Marketing Management*, No. 8 (New York: National Industrial Conference Board, 1965).

Company	SBU	Identifiable Competitor(s)
GE	Jet engines	Pratt & Whitney (United Technologies), Rolls Royce
GE	Home appliances	Amana (Raytheon), Maytag, Tappan, Whirlpool
Microsoft	Spread sheets	Lotus, Quattro, WordPerfect
ITT	Sheraton Hotels	Hilton, Holiday Inn, Marriott
GM	Trucks	Chrysler trucks, Ford trucks

Exhibit 6.3. Examples of SBUs.

attractiveness dimensions. These factors may vary by product line or industry. Exhibit 6.4 shows the sort of factors that may be used for each dimension. This two dimensional approach reflects the feeling of many strategic planners that a single measure (such as discounted cash flow) is inadequate to give the information needed for effective strategic planning.

When assessments of the business strength and industry attractiveness dimensions have been arrived at for all the SBUs, they are then plotted on a business screen similar to the one shown in Exhibit 6.5. The business screen is used to assign investment priorities to businesses or product lines. As typically drawn, there are three categories along each axis (high, medium and low) which result in a nine cell matrix, although more categories could be used on either dimension.[5] The resulting matrix is similar in concept to the four cell BCG matrix discussed earlier and is used in the same way.

Overall, an "invest" strategic assessment means an aggressive expansion of the unit's presence in the marketplace. A "selective investment" strategic assessment suggests that the current position should be maintained but monitored carefully. (This is roughly comparable to the "cash cow" of the four cell matrix, and may include many of the firm's traditional products.) A "harvest" strategic assessment suggests a controlled loss of position (including sale) to free up resources to use to assist units in the build category. The result of this analysis should be a cohesive corporate plan which is updated and reviewed each year.

---

5. For a description of a twelve-cell matrix, see Charles W. Hofer and Daniel Schendel, *Strategy Formulation: Analytical Concepts* (St. Paul, MN: West Publishing Company, 1978), pp. 30-34 and pp. 71–81.

Business Strength	Industry Attractiveness
Size	Size
Growth	Market growth rate
Share	Market diversity
Position	Competitive structure
Margins	Industry profitability
Technology positions	Technical role
Image	Social conditions
People	Environment
Location	Legal

Exhibit 6.4. Business strength and industry attractiveness factors.

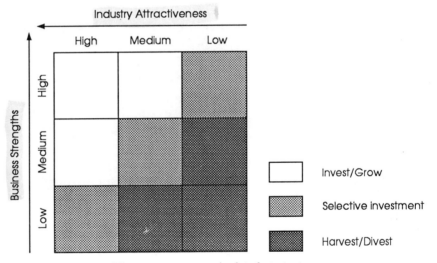

Exhibit 6.5. Typical business screen and related strategies.

The results for General Electric were excellent. The "profitless growth" of the 1960s was replaced with a steady growth in sales, earnings per share and return on equity during the 1970s. In 1981, Reginald Jones, Chairman of GE, was chosen as the best CEO in a survey of all the Fortune 500 CEOs. The excellent results obtained through use of the SBU concept undoubtedly played a large part in his selection.

When John F. Welch Jr. succeeded Jones in 1981, he expressed concern that the planning methods that GE pioneered in the 1960s and 1970s may have led to an undue emphasis on short term performance at the expense of long term gains and innovation.[6] Further, the elaborately developed plans weren't always followed by line managers. Consequently he reduced the corporate planning staff and placed much of the responsibility for planning back with the line managers. He also stressed that GE competed in world wide markets, and that its goal was to be first or second in each of the market segments it served, such as jet engines or medical systems.

More specifically, the multiple layers of management that had run the firm so successfully in the 1970s were increasingly seen as garbling communications and hobbling action. Consequently sectors, groups and much of the other management superstructure were dismantled during the 1980s to permit GE's businesses to move more quickly to take advantage of opportunities in a rapidly changing world. Today, GE only wants to be in businesses in which it can be first or second in its particular market. Other businesses are to be fixed, closed or sold. That explains why GE sold its housewares business to Black & Decker in 1984 and its RCA electronics business to Thomson of France in 1987.[7]

SUMMARY

The late 1960s and the 1970s were the heydays of corporate planning for diversified firms. The BCG and SBU concepts developed then are still used today in one form or another by almost all large, diversified companies. Further, such terms as cash cows, dogs and SBUs have become an established part of the manager's everyday vocabulary.

---

6. See Laura Landro, ''GE's Wizards Turning from the Bottom Line to Share of the Market,'' *The Wall Street Journal*, July 12, 1982, p.1. For more broad based criticisms of the SBU approach in hampering management's ability to manage global businesses, see Gary Hamel and C. K. Prahalad, ''Strategic Intent,'' *Harvard Business Review*, May–June 1989, pp. 63–76. In the authors' view, strategic intent is more than a statement of corporate strategy. It is an obsession with winning at all levels of the organization over a 10- to 20-year quest for global leadership.

7. Chairman John Welch's letters to shareholders in the Annual Reports for the 1980s provide an ongoing and very instructive discussion of the reasons GE changed the way it manages its businesses in the 1980s.

— 7 —

STRATEGY AND WAYS TO COMPETE

Selecting a corporate strategy implies selecting a way to compete for customers. It also implies answering the following questions about each product produced or service offered:

1. Who is our customer?
2. What is our product or service?
3. Why should the customer purchase the product or service from us?

We will now look at each of these questions in more detail.[1]

The first question—who is the customer?—incorporates a basic tenet of marketing into the strategy formulation process. We start with the customer to identify his or her needs. The second question—what is our product or service?—is closely related to the first. Certainly the product or service should satisfy one or more of the customer's needs. But there is an important point here that should not be overlooked. The needs should be identified *before* the product or service is developed. Many a firm has lost money (or gone out of business) because it developed a product it thought someone should want, but didn't. The Edsel automobile (1958), corfam shoes (late 1960s), and Qiana synthetic silk (1960s) are all examples of products that failed because they were developed and promoted before the need for them was established.

In contrast, most successful new consumer products are developed in response to a clearly evident need.[2] This is well illustrated in the field

---

1. This approach is consistent with Peter Drucker's assertion that the fundamental purpose of any business is to create a customer. See Peter F. Drucker, *The Practice of Management* (New York: Harper and Row, 1954), p. 37.

2. There is also evidence that most successful new products aren't developed through the formal research and development process at all. Rather, they come independently from the customer or from corporate personnel working to solve a customer's problem. See Thomas J. Peters and Robert H. Waterman, Jr., *In Search of Excellence* (New York: Harper & Row, 1982), pp. 193-195.

of photography. Although photography as we know it today was in existence by the time of the Civil War (1861–1865), it was a cumbersome procedure indeed. The camera's lens was literally a pin-hole in a box that permitted light to come through and form a "negative" image on a sensitized silver plate that needed to be processed chemically to produce a "positive" print.

In the late 1870s, George Eastman realized how absurd it was to have to carry trunk loads of equipment with him to take pictures on his planned vacation in the Caribbean. So he cancelled the trip and returned home to Rochester, New York where he concentrated on making it easier for the average person to take pictures. In 1884 he introduced a then-revolutionary new photographic product: film in rolls. The slogan of the Eastman Kodak Company (really its mission statement) became, "You press the button, we do the rest."[3] Today, Kodak is synonymous with easy to use, high quality photographic products designed primarily for the amateur photography market. (Professional photographers showed little interest in Eastman's attempts to simplify photography, hence his emphasis on the rapidly growing amateur photography market.)

A little more than a half century later, in 1943, Edmund Land was vacationing with his family at Santa Fe, New Mexico near the Grand Canyon when his daughter asked him, "Daddy, why do we have to wait so long to see the pictures we take?" Recognizing a customer need, Land persevered until he astounded the world of photography when he demonstrated the first instant photography camera in 1947. The original Polaroid Model 25 sold for $90 without film. In 1972 Polaroid introduced the SX70 camera, a technological marvel that folded into a one-quarter inch thick case and used a specially designed sonar device for automatic focusing. But this time Land was out of touch with his market; he had invented a product *he* liked. Customers did not want to pay $180 for his SX70, even if it did have a leather case and focused automatically. A year later, the leather case was replaced by a plastic one, the design itself was simplified, and the price was reduced to less than $100. Even so, the SX70 series of instant photography cameras never fulfilled the expectations Land and Polaroid had for it, and it was discontinued in 1980.

While it may occasionally be possible to create a demand for a product that was someone's pet idea or hobby, the odds of success are much greater if there is an intrinsic demand for the product. Consider the example of nylon stockings, made possible by the invention of nylon

---

3. Originally the customer sent the film *and* the camera to Kodak, where it was unloaded and processed. Kodak then re-loaded the camera and returned it to the customer. So the statement "You press the button, we do the rest" was literally true until Kodak made it possible for the customer to safely load and unload his or her own film.

by du Pont scientists under the direction of Dr. Wallace Carothers in 1938. First displayed at the New York World's Fair in 1939, they created an immediate sensation. When they went on sale in New York department stores on May 15, 1940 the entire stock of four million pair was bought up in a few hours! Not many products will achieve such immediate and lasting success, but the point is well taken: it is easier to sell a product the customer wants than one the customer doesn't want.

The third question—why should the customer buy the product or service from us?—leads directly to strategy formulation. Once the customer's need is identified, there may be several ways to meet that need. A firm must decide how it will compete and then develop plans and programs designed to make it appeal to prospective purchasers.

THE THREE BASIC WAYS TO COMPETE

When all is said and done, there are three basic ways, plus a few additional special ways, that a firm can compete to sell its goods or services.[4] The three basic ways are price, quality, and service (or delivery). All additional ways will be grouped into a fourth category called "other." As summarized in Exhibit 7.1, each basis of competition has one or more attributes associated with it that must be emphasized to attain success. Occasionally a product may compete on two bases at once (price and quality), but this is generally difficult to do for a prolonged period of time.

We will now look more closely at each of the three basic ways to compete.

1. Low Price

Competing on the basis of price means supplying the product or service desired at a cost equal to or lower than that of major competitors. Basic commodities such as steel, aluminum, coal and agricultural products usually compete on the basis of price. High volume permits firms in such industries to take advantage of economies of scale by having large plants and producing many thousands of tons or units per year. Price is the fundamental element of successful commodity competition. In recent years, severe price competition has arisen in such formerly regulated industries as air travel, banking and brokerage services. Price competition is also evident in consumer electronics (television sets, personal computers) and at the supermarket (colas, frozen foods, snack foods).

---

4. Ways to compete should not be confused with a firm's *distinctive competence*, that which it does unusually well. If a firm's distinctive competence is not in an area critical to a firm's success, it will do it little good.

Way to Compete	Key Attribute(s)	Examples
1 Low price	Volume	Kmart and Wal-Mart (retailing) Self-service gasoline stations Timex (watches)
2 Quality	Quality control	Leica (cameras) Mercedes-Benz (automobiles) Rolex (watches)
3 Delivery/service	Speed of delivery of product or service	Federal Express (air freight) McDonald's (fast food) Jiffy Print (copying service) Domino's (pizza)
4 Other	Patent protection	Xerox (plain paper copiers) Polaroid (instant photography)
	Creativity	Advertising agencies
	Geographic advantage	Dry cleaner, video rental store, gas station
	Status	Patek Philippe (watches) Rolls Royce (automobiles)
	Local monopoly	Billboard advertising rights Cable television franchise

Exhibit 7.1. Ways to compete, key attributes and examples.

For manufacturing firms, price competition implies close control of manufacturing costs (especially labor), use of modern equipment, and large plants to take advantage of economies of scale. It requires great discipline in controlling costs to compete on highly price sensitive items such as radios, television sets and watches where there is little noticeable difference in performance between brands. A Rolex watch with a traditional pin lever movement that sells for several thousand dollars actually does not keep as good time as a mass produced Seiko with a quartz movement that sells for less than a hundred dollars. As in the case of Seiko watches, the Japanese have clearly demonstrated that manufacturing efficiency can permit a firm to compete successfully by selling a good quality, low priced item in large quantities.

In the 1940s, Pepsi-Cola (now a division of PepsiCo) used price competition in an attempt to gain market share from Coca-Cola. This catchy jingle was used to highlight Pepsi's use of a twelve ounce bottle at the same price as Coke's traditional six-ounce size:

Pepsi-Cola hits the spot
Twelve full ounces, that's a lot
Twice as much for a nickel, too
Pepsi-Cola is the drink for you.

Price competition may also explicitly seek to take advantage of the "learning curve" effect, which means the labor cost per unit produced may decrease significantly with increased volume.[5] This is because the more often we do a task (even something as simple as washing dishes or putting up or taking down a folding table) the more efficient we become at it. According to this theory, the firm with the largest market share should be the low cost producer and consequently the most profitable in the industry. A major problem with this theory is that the largest producer is also usually the least flexible producer. Should production technology change rapidly, as in the semiconductor industry, the largest producer may find itself at the mercy of smaller producers who can more easily employ the newest production technology and produce at lower costs.

For a large retail or service business, price competition implies buying in large quantities, minimizing the use of expensive labor by emphasizing self-service, and locating close to major markets. Firms that purchase in very large quantities are able to obtain the manufacturer's lowest price and can also minimize shipping and handling costs per unit. A policy of many retailing firms such as Kmart, Sears and Wal-Mart is to never knowingly be undersold by any competitor in the area.

Some firms go a step further and guarantee to meet the lower price for six months or a year *after* the sale has been made. Highland Superstores, a midwest discounter of name brand electronic goods and home appliances, has a low price guarantee for the life of the product. If a customer purchases an item and later finds it for sale anywhere at a lower price, Highland will refund the difference.

Retailing firms may also engage in private branding, where they sell a name brand product at a lower price under their own name. For years, Sears Roebuck has sold home appliances made by Whirlpool under its own Kenmore name. The primary difference between a Whirlpool and a Kenmore home appliance is the name tag; both are made on the same assembly line. Private branding also allows the manufacturer to spread overhead over a larger volume of output, hence reducing the manufacturing costs of its own brand of products. (The agreement between Sears and Whirlpool is not written down, but is referred to as "the handshake across the lake," reflecting the fact that Sears headquarters are in Chicago on the southwestern part of Lake Michigan and Whirlpool headquarters are in Benton Harbor, Michigan, on the lake's eastern shore.)

2. Quality

Products or services that compete on the basis of quality are designed to fit the needs of customers for whom price is not the major consideration.

---

5. See, for example, Winfred B. Hirschman, "Profit from the Learning Curve," *Harvard Business Review*, January-February 1964, pp. 125–129.

Although initially higher in price, such products may prove to be less expensive in the long run than a lower priced but lower quality product. Florsheim Imperial shoes cost about $150 a pair, but with reasonable care they can last several times longer than most competing brands. Here the criterion becomes cost per time used or worn, not just the initial cost. A family may pay a higher price for Maytag appliances for their home, but consider them a good value because they give more years of trouble-free service than less expensive competing brands. So, too, people may buy Budweiser beer, Heinz ketchup or Pepperidge Farm bread because they think the quality of the product is worth its premium price.

Margins on high quality goods are generally considerably higher than on goods which compete on the basis of price. Use may be a more important criterion to the customer than cost for these products: how long they will last or how long they will perform, not how much they cost initially, is the determining factor. McIntosh audio products have been the industry leader since McIntosh Laboratories was founded in Binghampton, New York, in 1953. Although very expensive, their products reflect quality throughout. Their rigid construction, conservative specifications and low power consumption have combined to create a loyal following of satisfied McIntosh owners.

A good way to tell whether a product is perceived to be of high quality is to check its resale value, or see how often used units are offered for sale. McIntosh stereo equipment is rarely seen on the used equipment shelf in audio stores or in the classified advertisements. Similarly, a Mercedes-Benz seldom lasts long on a used car lot and consistently sells for a premium compared to American automobiles. A decision to compete on quality generally implies that products won't be mass produced and that each product will be carefully inspected and tested before being shipped from the factory to the dealer.[6]

3. Service or Delivery

Firms that compete on service or delivery usually strive to fill a specific need at a moment when time of delivery is the most important concern of the customer. Thus a freeway traveler expects to pay more for a gallon of gas or a meal at a service area in return for having the service area open, safe and clean regardless of the time of day or night.

---

6. We often overlook the miracle of quality inherent in the mass production of such items as automobiles and television sets. The General Motors 350 V-8 automobile engine is legendary for long life and minimal maintenance. Stories abound of car owners who have driven these engines 200,000 miles and more without major repair, about twice the average for car engines as a whole. Sony television sets commonly last ten years or more without repair, and then the most common repair before soft touch switches became standard was replacement of the rotary mechanical channel selector. Thus mass production and quality can go together, but we generally think of a quality product as one made with better materials and to finer tolerances without any compromise in design.

70

A steel service center makes its money by acting as a buffer between the mills and customers who need steel quickly. The steel service center buys mill overruns and keeps them in inventory. Then in return for a premium price, it will provide prompt (often one day) delivery of reasonably large quantities of a wide variety of steel.

Air freight forwarders such as Airborne Freight, Emery Air Freight and Federal Express guarantee overnight delivery of small packages to most larger cities in the United States but charge a premium for this service. Often the customer finds it more to his or her advantage to have the package delivered quickly than to save a small amount in shipping charges.[7]

Delivery has become a primary means of competition in the fast food industry. The time between placing an order and receiving the food is minimized by having many places to order inside and one or more drive-up windows outside. Domino's Pizza has taken the concept of delivery one step further. It doesn't sell pizzas to be eaten on premises, but delivers them to your residence at no charge.[8]

SPECIAL WAYS TO COMPETE

All other ways to compete are grouped under this heading, since they usually require some special circumstance to make them workable. Here are four examples of special ways to compete.

Patent Protection

Polaroid (instant photography) and Xerox (copiers) are examples of firms that were granted significant advantages over their competitors for the life of their patents. For such firms, patents are granted as a reward for successful research and development efforts.

Location

A good location may provide a natural competitive advantage. Consider the desirability of having a fast food franchise near Disneyland or a dry cleaning establishment outside the gate of a major military base.

---

7. Occasionally a slower than normal delivery in return for a lower delivery charge is a basis of competition. A customer may elect to mail printed matter by book rate, not caring that it will take a week or more to be delivered.

8. As lower priced cellular telephone technology makes it feasible for more cars to have phones, it may soon be possible to call your order in to your favorite fast food restaurant ahead of time from your car so it will be waiting for you when you arrive. That would be the ultimate in fast food service!

Status

Sometimes a product can compete on the basis of status alone. Such products don't perform a task appreciably better than products less than half their price, but the fact that they are so expensive and widely advertised makes them desirable as status symbols to some people. Selected watch companies advertise in magazines such as *The New Yorker* hoping to entice affluent readers to buy their wares. A Patek Philippe or Rolex watch for several thousand dollars may not keep any better time than a hundred dollar mass produced Seiko, but it does say something about the financial standing of the person wearing it. An advertisement for a Patek Philippe, one of the world's most expensive watches, is shown in Exhibit 7.2.

Exhibit 7.2. Advertisement for a Patek Philippe watch. **Source:** Tourneau Corner, 1988. (Reprinted with permission.)

Legal Decision

Occasionally a legal decision can work to a firm's benefit. In a 1962 lawsuit between Pepsi-Cola and Dr Pepper, the court found that Dr Pepper was not a cola drink like Pepsi-Cola and Coca-Cola, and hence could be bottled as a flavor line by both Pepsi-Cola and Coca-Cola bottlers. This gave Dr Pepper immediate nationwide distribution at minimal cost and led directly to its rapid growth in the next decade.

APPLICATION TO CONSUMER GOODS

Makers of consumer goods such as clothing or food products often have considerable leeway to decide how they will compete. One choice is to compete on the basis of price alone and sell basically a generic product. Very few firms elect to compete this way. Most firms try to build *brand names* for their products, usually through the use of advertising. Probably the most basic consumer goods marketing strategy is to attempt to make an undifferentiated (generic) product such as beer, crackers or salt that could sell on the basis of price alone sell at a higher price on the basis of perceived quality.[9] This is usually done by advertising, which attempts to associate an image of quality with the brand name of the product. The idea is to get the consumer to ask for *Miller* beer, *Morton* salt or *Bayer* aspirin rather than simply beer, salt or aspirin, all also sold in generic form at lower prices. In the 1960s and 1970s, Heublein Corporation (now a part of Grand Metropolitan PLC) spent about ten percent of sales, twice the liquor industry average, to establish Smirnoff as the leading vodka and one of the top selling liquor brands. Heublein in turn charged a premium price for Smirnoff to obtain the high margins necessary to sustain its unusually high advertising expenditures.

Exhibit 7.3 shows the twenty firms that spent the most on advertising in 1990. The top 100 advertisers spent a total of $35.6 billion. These large firms spend heavily on advertising in an attempt to set their products apart in the eyes of the consumer from very similar products made by their competitors. Note that all the firms listed in Exhibit 7.3 are primarily producers of consumer goods rather than industrial or military goods.

Heavy advertising to establish a brand name opens up an alternative strategy for smaller firms: selling a low cost "look alike" version of a heavily advertised brand name product. L. Perrigo specializes in making

---

9. Theodore Levitt argues in *The Marketing Imagination* (New York: The Free Press, 1983) that it is possible to differentiate virtually any product in the eye of the consumer. See especially Chapter 4, "Differentiation—of Anything."

TWENTY LARGEST ADVERTISERS, 1990

Rank	Company	Amount	Sales	% of Sales
1	Procter & Gamble	$2,285	$27,026	8.5%
2	Philip Morris	2,210	51,169	4.3
3	Sears, Roebuck	1,507	55,972	2.7
4	General Motors	1,503	124,705	1.2
5	Grand Metropolitan PLC	883	16,616	5.3
6	PepsiCo	849	17,803	4.8
7	AT&T	797	37,285	2.1
8	McDonald's	764	6,640	11.5
9	Kmart	693	32,070	2.2
10	Time Warner	677	11,517	5.9
11	Eastman Kodak	665	18,908	3.5
12	Johnson & Johnson	654	11,232	5.8
13	RJR Nabisco	636	13,879	4.6
14	Nestle SA	636	36,511	1.7
15	Warner-Lambert	631	4,687	13.5
16	Ford Motor Company	616	97,650	.6
17	Toyota	581	71,400	.8
18	Kellogg	578	5,181	11.2
19	Unilever NV	569	39,620	1.4
20	General Mills	539	7,153	7.5

Exhibit 7.3. Twenty largest advertisers, 1990. (Dollar amounts in $000,000s). Adapted from *Advertising Age*, September 25, 1991.

low cost, private brand versions of such products as hand lotion, soap and shampoo. These products contain virtually the same ingredients as the name brand product (often the ingredients are identical) but sell at a substantial discount. Retailers (Kmart) and drug store chains (Walgreen's) also like these private brand products. They offer about twice the margins national brands do because there is minimal advertising expenditure associated with them.[10] Large firms may also make private brands. 3M is the largest maker of private brand photographic film, such as Focal, which it makes for Kmart. Whirlpool makes home apliances for Sears under the Kenmore name, and Sharp makes home electronics for Montgomery Ward under the Signature name.

TWO WAYS AT THE SAME TIME

Occasionally a product can emphasize two of the basic ways to compete at the same time, although this is generally difficult to do for a sustained period of time. Here are two examples of firms that have been able to do this successfully.

Lincoln Electric

Lincoln's arc welders are famous for their high quality and low price. Their stringent attention to cost control and emphasis on high quality has caused such firms as General Electric to leave the welder field, a remarkable achievement given General Electric's fine reputation as a manufacturer of industrial products.

Kmart and Wal-Mart

Since its first store opened in Detroit in 1962, Kmart has offered brand name merchandise at low prices, thus attempting to compete on quality and price. Its main competitors (at the time,) Sears, J.C. Penney, and Montgomery Ward, took pride in offering most merchandise in their stores under their own brand names. Recently all three of these stores have followed the Kmart lead and now offer brand name merchandise of known quality at discount prices. Wal-Mart Stores, the country's fastest growing retailer, modeled its very successful retailing business on the Kmart concept. Wal-Mart's founder, Sam Walton, was so impressed when

---

10. By law the ingredients of each product must be given on its container. Ingredients are listed in descending order by weight or volume, but the percentage that each ingredient represents does not need to be given. When the ingredients on a brand name toothpaste or hand lotion are compared to a quality private brand of the same product, chances are very good that the ingredients will be identical.

he visited one of the first Kmart stores in 1962 that he used many of its features in his Wal-Mart stores.

The reason that most products compete on only one dimension is straightforward. If profits are high, then capital will flow to that product area, output will increase to meet demand and prices will fall. If a firm can compete on two dimensions for a long period of time, is it usually due to an unusual combination of circumstances. Lincoln Electric can compete on both price and quality because its labor force is twice as productive as that of its major competitors. This is due to a unique wage incentive system whereby its hourly employees can earn twice as much as most factory workers if they are willing to work hard.

Well run firms in industries where there are no unusual barriers to entry such as patent protection, geographical advantage or threats of adverse legislation will usually have an after tax return on equity ranging from fifteen to twenty percent. This reflects the firm's ability to perform well in a situation where competitors are free to come and go as they see attractive opportunities to invest capital.

SUMMARY

For each of its products, a firm should be able to give good answers to the three basic questions:

1. Who is our customer?
2. What is our product or service?
3. Why should the customer purchase the product or service from us?

Once these questions have been satisfactorily answered, the firm needs to determine on what basis each product or service will compete. Except in unusual cases, a product will compete on the basis of price, quality or delivery. A firm that does a good job of formulating a product strategy should expect to earn an after tax return on equity of between fifteen and twenty percent on that product. The corporate strategy for a single or related product firm should be the summation of the individual product strategies, and should be stated so it reflects the commonality inherent in the individual product strategies. In the multi-product firm or a conglomerate, there will have to be a set of strategies, one for each major business area. And in such firms it is quite possible that different products will compete on different bases of competition.

Strategic Discontinuities: When Being Good May Not Be Enough

by Henry H. Beam

A decade ago few would have predicted that by 1990 Apple, Compaq, and Microsoft would be the success stories of the computer industry, not IBM. Similarly, few would have thought that Sears, the world's largest retailer for over half a century, would be struggling for survival while two relative newcomers, Kmart and Wal-Mart, would be on their way to overtaking Sears. Yet that is exactly what has happened.

Sears and IBM are classic examples of what happens when a successful firm is confronted by a *strategic discontinuity,* a special type of challenge to corporate strategy that can render a successful strategy ineffective. It occurs when a firm is faced with a competitor that has found a better way to provide the same goods or services, usually using a different way to compete.

Ways to Compete

There are three basic ways to compete: on the basis of delivery (including convenience), quality (including service), or price. Commodities and undifferentiated products (beer, gasoline, sugar) tend to sell on the basis of price. Brand name products (automobiles, clothing, food) sell on the basis of perceived quality and the promise of the manufacturer to stand behind the product. IBM and Caterpillar (construction machinery) are legendary for providing support for the their customers worldwide. Advertising can be use to make an inherently undifferentiated product into a brand name, such as Coca-Cola soft drinks, Heinz ketchup, or Morton salt. Delivery becomes important when the customer wants the product right away (fast food, instant printing) and does not mind paying a premium price for the prompt service. McDonald's is known the world over for its quick service, and has sold over 70 billion hamburgers as a result.

Profit margins, or return on sales, are closely related to the basis of competition used. When an item is a commodity, profit margins are low (less than 3 percent) and profitability is attained through high volume, as at self-serve gas stations or grocery stores. When an item has a brand name associated with it, acceptable profitability can be attained with medium margins (3 to 8 percent) and medium volume. This is particularly true of products that undergo periodic model changes or product improvement, such as automobiles, pharmaceutical products, or television sets. Advertising is used extensively to convince the customer that he or she is buying a Buick or a Taurus, not merely basic transportation. Convenience items (snack foods, Post-it note pads) are usually sold in small amounts so the customer does not mind paying a premium price. Here high margins compensate for low volume. This is also true of large, one-of-a-kind projects (the space shuttle, new buildings) where on-time completion according to specifications is often more important than price.

Figure 1 shows a nine-cell matrix drawn with profit margins on the vertical axis and volume on the horizontal axis. The three basic ways to compete—delivery/convenience, quality/service, and price—and their associated normal profit margins plot along the diagonal from upper left to lower right. The product of profit margin and volume in each of these positions provides adequate levels of profitability to sustain a business. Most firms that have been successful for many years fall naturally into one of these three positions.

The three cells beneath the diagonal line in Figure 1 should be avoided. They represent situations where profitability is too low to sustain a business. The brokerage industry and the air transport industry (both now deregulated) fall into the low-margin/medium-volume cell. Volume can be gained by reducing prices (price wars), but overall profitability is still unsatisfactory. Profit margins in the air transport industry as a whole averaged less than 1 percent from 1984 to 1989, a dismal performance. Many small businesses fail because they are unable to break out of the low-volume/low-profit cell, the worst of all situations.

Gaining Temporary Advantage

Figure 1 also shows how desirable it would be to compete at a point above the diagonal, since this would result in increased profitability, either through increased margins, increased volume, or both. Two of America's most successful companies, Sears and IBM, found ways to do that for sustained periods of time. But both struggled throughout the 1980s to maintain their leadership positions.

Sears

Long the dominant American retailing firm, Sears could have chosen to compete almost exclusively on price years ago. It forsook this option for one it perceived to be more profitable: put the Sears brand name on its products, advertise that brand name, and charge a higher price. Sears used this strategy to develop a large base of loyal customers who associated the Sears brand name with value in everything from screwdrivers to shirts. Sears sought to maintain the medium margins associated with

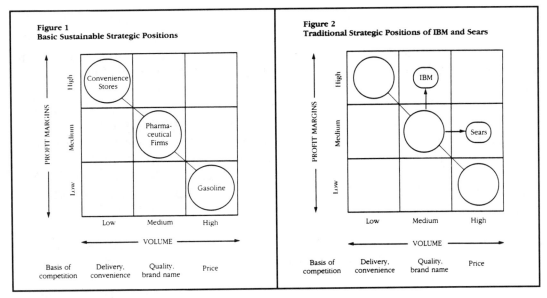

Figure 1. Basic Sustainable Strategic Positions

Figure 2. Traditional Strategic Positions of IBM and Sears

brand name merchandise and still develop the high volume usually associated with items that sell primarily on the basis of price. For more than 50 years Sears was very successful in competing at the position to the right of the diagonal line shown in **Figure 2**. Its average profit margins of 5 percent were about 50 percent higher than the industry average.

Sears would have been happy to compete this way forever. But by the 1980s Sears was becoming an unhappy victim of a strategic discontinuity that would require it to change its traditional way of doing business if it wished to remain the world's largest retailer. The threat to Sears' supremacy did not come from Ward's, its principal rival for 50 years. It started unnoticed in 1959 when Harry B. Cunningham became president of S. S. Kresge & Company, a Detroit-based dime store chain. Cunningham envisioned a new type of store, to be called a Kmart, that would feature name brand merchandise at discount prices all the time. Advertising was not directed at establishing a Kmart brand to compete directly with the Sears brand. Its purpose was to make the Kmart name synonymous in customers' minds with name brand merchandise at discount prices, something not previously available to them. It thus shifted the basis of competition from quality (as implied in the Sears brand name) to price (name brands available at a discount).

The new strategy was so successful that S. S. Kresge soon concentrated on opening Kmart stores nationwide, closing most of its dime stores in the process. In 1977, the transformation complete, it changed its name to Kmart. The shrewdest observer of this change was not Sears or Montgomery Ward, but Sam Walton. He used the Kmart concept to perfection in developing his Wal-Mart Stores into the nation's fastest-growing firm.

By the 1980s Sears could no longer ignore the strategic discontinuity brought on by the Kmart concept. It had to rethink its basic strategy. To remain the same (emphasizing the Sears brand) would almost certainly result in continued loss of market share and profitability, and could possibly lead to a hostile takeover. Sears' only other real choice was to change to price as its primary way to compete, moving downward so it would again be on the diagonal in Figure 2. This, in fact, is what Sears chose to do, even though it meant going head-to-head with Kmart and Wal-Mart. On March 1, 1989, Sears closed all 824 of its stores to re-price 50,000 items and implement is name-brand merchandise and every-day low-pricing strategy.

Sears' crisis did not occur because of lack of effort or inattention on the part of management but because Sears refused to accept that Kmart and Wal-Mart had developed a better way to provide what the customer wanted. Sears could have easily made an uncontested move to competing on the basis of price years ago; this position was vacant until the opening of the first Kmart store in 1962. Instead, Sears continued its old strategy until the mid-1980s, when the loss of share caused by the strategic discontinuity became so great that it could no longer be ignored.

IBM

International Business Machines, or IBM as it is universally known, is one of the great business success stories of all time. Few firms have so dominated a market as IBM has computers, garnering market shares of 70 percent from the 1950s through the 1970s. Yet IBM, still the colossus of the industry with 1989 revenues of $62.7 billion, is also facing a crisis. Sales growth has slowed, but even worse, its traditionally high profit margins have eroded from about 14 percent in 1980 to less than 10 percent today.

Like Sears, IBM had perfected a strategy for a market that is rapidly disappearing. IBM's natural competitive position was in the middle of the matrix in Figure 1, selling medium volumes of brand name computers at medium margins. But years ago IBM perceived it could improve its profitability by moving above the diagonal line. Unlike Sears, which moved to the right, IBM moved upward as shown in Figure 2. IBM used its reputation for realibility and outstanding service to sell its products to corporate executives who felt secure with IBM equipment, even if it came at a premium price and was not always on the leading edge of technology. Its large customer base provided a ready source of prospects for each new generation of computing equipment.

IBM's strategy was sound and its implementation was virtually flawless. It routinely fended off all who tried to compete head-on with it. (General Electric and RCA are two firms that tried and failed.) As with Sears, the strategic discontinuity that IBM faces today was not the result of a traditional competitor's action. It started in 1977 in a California garage 2,500 miles from IBM's Armonk, New York headquarters when college dropouts Steve Jobs and Steve Wosniak started Apple Computer. Even though IBM introduced its own personal computer in 1981 and soon set the standard for the industry, the PC did not fit easily into its traditional line of high-margin mainframe computing systems sold by its legendary sales force. The personal computer didn't change what a computer could do, but it did change who would use it (professionals, not data processing experts), where they would use it (on their desk or at home, not in the data processing center), and where they would buy it (from the local computer store or at a discount through a purchase plan where they worked, not from an IBM sales representative).

This came as a major shock to the stable world of IBM, especially since the performance of the PC improved so quickly that it was soon able to do jobs that hitherto could only be done on a mainframe. The strategic discontinuity that caused IBM's crisis arose from how the increasingly popular PCs would be sold. Once it became apparent that all PCs contained virtually the same components regardless of brand name, price, not service, became the primary selling point.

Today the personal computer sells like a commodity—on the basis of price. Brand loyalty is minimal in the face of substantially lower prices offered by a competitor. Like Sears, IBM does not like its present strategic choices. If it continues to emphasize larger mainframe systems, it is competing in the industry's slowest growth segment. If it moves its strategic position to selling high volumes of low-priced computers with low margins, it would lose much of the value of the IBM brand name. It would also be abandoning the strategy that had worked so well in the past. Yet PCs are the future of the computer industry, accounting for more than 90 percent of unit sales and over one-third of dollar sales in 1988. Since Apple, Compaq, and other firms have already staked out significant positions in the high-volume/low-margin field, IBM will have difficulty dominating the PC market the way it dominates the mainframe market.

The Lesson

The lesson from these examples is that even very successful strategies need to be periodically reviewed to see if they are still appropriate.

Strategic discontinuities are like flash floods and tornadoes: they don't happen very often, but when they do, they can have devastating consequences. How does a firm identify possible strategic discontinuities? First it must understand that a strategic discontinuity is not the same as the more common technological breakthrough. The pocket calculator made the slide rule obsolete, and the diesel engine replaced steam as the source of power for locomotives. But the new products were marketed to the same customers in the same way as the old products.

Technological breakthroughs are an accepted part of business and their impact can often be estimated from an analysis of trends. A strategic discontinuity may include a technological breakthrough, but its distinguishing characteristic is that it incorporates a shift to a new base of competition, often from quality and service to price.

In the 1950s fishing reels were precision instruments made to last a lifetime by companies such as Pflueger, Shakespeare, and South Bend. The new spinning reel not only offered superior performance (especially by virtually eliminating backlashes when casting) but also could be mass produced at lower cost. When a combination spinning rod and reel sells for less than $10, reliability and service cease to be major selling points. It is easier to buy a new set than to repair an old one. The basis for selling fishing equipment has shifted from quality to price.

Anticipating Strategic Discontinuities

Strategic discontinuities must be anticipated; they can't be identified from trends alone because, unlike trends, they represent a break from what was done in the past, not a projection of the past into the future. Intuition and sharp peripheral vision are the key skills in anticipating strategic discontinuities.

The Kmart strategy proposed by Harry B. Cunningham is a textbook example of anticipating and taking advantage of a strategic discontinuity. Instead of being preoccupied with the F. W. Woolworth Company, S. S. Kresge's major competitor, Cunningham took a much broader look at changes in American society. He found that by the late 1950s Kresge's traditional customers were moving from large cities to the suburbs and wanted name brand merchandise, including appliances and other big-ticket items, at discount prices. In the late 1950s no one had a store like that. Like Woolworth's, all of Kresge's stores were in downtown locations and sold—as the dime store name implied—inexpensive merchandise. By being the first to identify a strategic discontinuity, Cunningham could move S. S. Kresge into a new competitive position virtually uncontested.

The Kmart example shows how important it is to look beyond the likely actions of competitors to identify strategic discontinuities. A series of "what if" questions appropriate to the firm and its industry can prompt thinking about the possible sources of future strategic discontinuities. Here are three examples of such questions:

1. What if the *performance* of our product was improved so much that customers would be willing to pay a premium for it? Example: the compact disk, which virtually eliminates distortion, as a way to play music rather than records or tapes.

2. What if the *reliability* of our product was improved so much that service was no longer essential? Example: steel-belted radial tires that regularly last 50,000 miles or more, compared to their rayon predecessors that average 15,000 miles a set.

3. What if *new technology* permitted our product to give the same (or higher) level of performance at a much lower price? Example: the quartz movement watch replacing the mechanical pin-lever watch. The quartz movement has fewer parts, provides greater accuracy, and is much less expensive to manufacture.

Remember that strategic discontinuities arise because of a fundamental shift in the way a firm competes. Once identified, they seem obvious, yet they may have gone undetected for years. Better distribution techniques together with volume purchasing made it possible for Kmart and Wal-Mart to sell name brand products at discount prices. New firms such as Apple and Compaq that specialized in personal computers encouraged the growth of computer stores that catered as much to individuals as to corporate accounts, and now account for over 80 percent of all PCs sold.

IBM's sales force, long its pride and joy, was of little competitive advantage in persuading an individual to buy an IBM PC when a clone could be purchased for considerably less. Even IBM's reputation for service was of little use in this new market. The PCs were very reliable, but more important, they cost much less than the mainframes they increasingly replaced. Repairability and service were no longer major concerns of the customer (or selling points for the maker) when buying the product.

Responses

A firm faced with a strategic discontinuity generally has three responses available to it:

- Sell on the basis of price. Strive for high volume because margins are lower on items that sell primarily on the basis of price. High volume also implies being able to produce at the lowest possible cost, which helps compensate for the lower margins. This is the alternative Sears has chosen.

- Sell on the basis of brand name and charge a premium price. This is how Alfred P. Sloan countered Henry Ford's strategy of selling the same car at even lower prices in the 1920s. Sloan developed a hierarchy of brand names at General Motors (Chevrolet, Pontiac, Oldsmobile, Buick, Cadillac) that gave the customer a choice of features and styles; he was able to charge a higher price in the process. This also appears to be the alternative IBM is choosing, although it may be harder to differentiate computers than automobiles in a customer's mind.
- Sell on the basis of superior performance. Strive for high margins, not the mass market. This is the alternative Rolex selected when quartz watches that kept perfect time were mass marketed by Seiko and Timex for prices well under $100. Rolex continued to make pin-lever movements, emphasized the durability of its one-piece steel or gold cases, and priced its watches from $1,000 up to appeal to customers on the basis of status and quality rather than accuracy. Rolex has been very successful in convincing its customers they are buying a fine piece of jewelry, not just a watch.

The response a firm selects will depend on its own values and the size of the markets it serves. Rolex and Seiko are both very successful in the watch industry, but they have taken very different paths in response to the strategic discontinuity brought about by the accuracy and low cost of the quartz-movement watch. Old-line watch firms such as Hamilton and Longines never imagined a watch could be made that kept perfect time, had few moving parts, and sold for less than ten dollars. Yet that is exactly what was done in the 1970s, and by electronics firms, not established watchmakers. Most makers of traditional pin-lever watches didn't formulate any strategy to deal with this strategic discontinuity and consequently went out of business.

We have already seen how two historically very successful firms, IBM and Sears, were adversely affected by strategic discontinuities when they failed to alter their traditional strategies. Strategic discontinuities are particularly traumatic for firms that have been market leaders for long periods of time. Most executives find it extremely difficult to change what has been a winning strategy. The easiest course is often to simply fine-tune the old strategy or concentrate on better implementation. It is also tempting to restrict the analysis of competitive threats only to direct competitors, as Sears did with Ward's. But as the examples of Sears and IBM demonstrate, even very successful strategies need to be carefully reviewed at least annually to make sure they aren't vulnerable to a strategic discontinuity.☐

References

Brian Bremmer and Michael Oneal. "The Big Store's Big Trauma," *Business Week*, July 10, 1989, pp. 50–51, 54–55.

Geoff Lewis, "Big Changes at Big Blue," *Business Week*, February 15, 1988, pp. 92–98.

Carol J. Loomis. "IBM's Big Blues: A Legend Tries to Remake Itself," *Fortune*, January 19, 1987, pp. 34–36, 40, 44, 48, 52, 54.

Patricia Sellers. "Why Bigger is Badder at Sears," *Fortune*, December 5, 1988, pp. 79–84.

━━ 8 ━━

R&D AND CORPORATE STRATEGY

The importance of research and development (R&D) is self-evident. Without spending some of its earnings each year on R&D, a company won't develop any new products on which to build its future. However, in practice, general managers typically know very little about R&D or the way it relates to a firm's strategy. Thus a review of the difference between the two basic types of research, pure and applied, may be helpful.

Pure research refers to the discovery of new knowledge. In its most basic form, it is done without any preconceived idea of future applications. Only the largest, best financed corporations, such as AT&T and IBM, can afford the luxury of pure research. Probably the best example of a firm that has done pure research for many years is the Bell Telephone Laboratories, where over one hundred engineers and scientists are free to work on projects of their own choosing. This great concentration of talent, plus a virtually unlimited budget, has permitted Bell Laboratories to develop a multitude of state of the art devices.

The best known of these inventions, and the one with the greatest impact on our lives, was the transistor. In 1947, the research team of Bardeen, Brattain and Shockley succeeded in developing a solid state device that would amplify current. (The vacuum tube, in contrast, is a voltage amplification device.) Although the applications of this new device could only begin to be imagined, the transistor and its descendants, the integrated circuit and the silicon chip, have changed the way we live. They have made possible the high speed digital computer, which was essential for the space program, and have been applied to a wide array of electronic products ranging from portable radios to television sets to pocket calculators. Probably none of these applications was clearly envisioned when the transistor was invented.

Few firms have the resources to do pure research on an ongoing basis, and the results of the research rarely have the impact of the transistor. Thus when most firms speak of research, they are really referring to *applied research,* or development, as it is also called. Development refers to the application of existing scientific knowledge to the solution of specific problems, often for a particular customer.

Research and development expenditures are usually lumped together for purposes of reporting to shareholders. However, knowing what type of business a firm is in often permits making a good guess about the nature of expenditures listed as R&D. Thus at the Upjohn Company, a leading maker of pharmaceutical products, most of the R&D expenditures are probably for pure research in the hope of discovering a new drug that could have an enormous payoff for the company. At Whirlpool Corporation, on the other hand, the R&D expenditures are probably primarily for applied research to find ways to adapt new technology to existing products. For example, when soft-touch control switches were perfected, they were integrated into existing product lines to make them easier to use.

R&D SPENDING AND CORPORATE STRATEGY

The first question that should always be asked is, "Do we need R&D, and if so, how much?" Most executives will instinctively respond "Of course we do." But a closer look will show that R&D expenditures should match a firm's strategy, and not be arbitrarily set at some predetermined amount such as five percent of sales. The range of R&D expenditures for large corporations generally runs from less than one percent to slightly above ten percent of sales. A *Business Week* survey of 900 firms in thirty-nine industry groups showed they spent an average of 3.6% of sales on R&D in 1991.[1] Exhibit 8.1 shows how much the top ten firms in the survey spent.

A look at Exhibit 8.2 shows that R&D expenses as a percent of sales do vary considerably by industry and suggests that the nature of a firm's business might be enough to determine its appropriate R&D strategy. Thus a technology based firm such as Hewlett-Packard would be expected to spend a great deal on R&D, while a consumer goods firm such as Kellogg would not. However, this is not necessarily so. While it is true that IBM spends an enormous amount on R&D in absolute terms ($5.0 billion in 1991), it is not usually considered a technological leader in the computer business. Smaller computer firms such as Apple, Compaq,

---

1. "On a Clear Day You Can See Progress," *Business Week*, June 29, 1992, p. 104.

LEADING R&D SPENDERS

		R&D	Sales	R&D as % of Sales	R&D per Employee
1	General Motors	$5,887	$122,081	4.8%	$ 7,785
2	IBM	5,001	64,792	7.7	14,515
3	Ford Motor Company	3,728	88,286	4.2	11,205
4	AT&T	3,114	44,651	7.0	9,820
5	Digital Equipment	1,649	13,911	11.9	13,631
6	Eastman Kodak	1,494	19,419	7.7	11,216
7	Hewlett-Packard	1,463	14,494	10.1	16,438
8	Boeing	1,417	29,314	4.8	9,101
9	General Electric	1,402	59,379	2.4	4,937
10	du Pont	1,298	38,151	3.4	9,791

Exhibit 8.1. Top ten companies in R&D spending, 1991. (Dollar figures in $000,000s). Adapted from *Business Week,* June 29, 1992, p. 105–123.

Digital Equipment and Hewlett-Packard do not spend nearly as much on an absolute basis as IBM does because they don't have the resources to do so. In fact, as shown in Exhibit 8.3, IBM's R&D expenditures of $5.0 billion are not far from Apple's 1991 sales of $6.3 billion. Yet Apple, Compaq, Digital Equipment and Hewlett-Packard are the firms that have innovated. Apple introduced the personal computer in 1978, Compaq developed high performance portable computers, Digital pioneered the use of mini-computers, and Hewlett-Packard developed the first high powered hand held electronic calculator. But because of its size ($64.8 billion in sales in 1991) and large share of the computer market, IBM often sets the standard for the industry as it did when it introduced its Personal Computer (PC) in 1980.

Industry	R&D as % of Sales, 1991
Software & services	13.5%
Drugs & research	10.8
Computers	8.8
Electrical & electronics	5.8
Automotive	4.2
Chemicals	4.1
Telecommunications	4.0
Aerospace	3.8
Manufacturing	2.9
Consumer products	1.4
Metals and mining	1.3
Paper & forest products	1.0
Fuel	0.8
Food	0.7

Exhibit 8.2. R&D as a percent of sales and per employee, selected industries, 1991. Adapted from *Business Week*, R&D Scoreboard, June 29, 1992.

BASIC R&D STRATEGIES

There are three basic R&D strategies that industrial firms can follow:[2]

1. Innovation

Firms that constantly seek to innovate such as Hewlett-Packard, Minnesota Mining and Manufacturing (3M) and Upjohn will spend a large percentage of sales on R&D annually.

---

2. Firms in service industries such as fast food or retailing generally spend well under one percent of sales on R&D, although new products or new ways of delivering those products may be just as important to them as to industrial firms. Advertising (discussed in Chapter 7) is often as important or more important to these firms as R&D.

	Sales	R&D expenditures	R&D as % of Sales
IBM	$64,792	$5,001	7.7%
Digital Equipment	13,911	1,649	11.9
Hewlett-Packard	14,494	1,463	10.1
Apple Computer	6,309	583	9.2
Compaq Computer	3,271	197	6.0

Exhibit 8.3. R&D expenditures as a percent of sales, five computer manufacturers, 1991. Adapted from *Business Week*, R&D Scoreboard, June 29, 1992, p. 120. Dollar amounts in millions.

These firms depend on a constant stream of new products for future sales as present product lines become obsolete or patent protection expires. The life cycle of a new product may only be a few years, so the firm needs a steady stream of new products to prosper and grow. Highly innovative firms will typically spend between 7–10% of sales on R&D each year. Most drug companies follow this R&D strategy. In 1991 the Upjohn Company spent 14.0% of its sales of $3.4 billion, or $491 million, for R&D.

2. Monitoring Technology

This strategy may be described as "let someone else invent it, then we will perfect it." It is the antithesis of the strategy of constant innovation. While this strategy may lack glamour, it has the advantages of lower cost and reduced risk. A good example of a firm that uses this R&D strategy as its corporate strategy is L. Perrigo, which makes private brands of popular consumer goods such as hand lotion and shampoo. A Fortune 500 firm that has used this approach to R&D with great success is Crown Cork & Seal Corporation. Unlike American Can and Continental Can, its two much larger competitors that built their own R&D centers, Crown Cork & Seal concentrated instead on monitoring developments in technology such as the aluminum can and the "snap-top" beer and soft drink can opener. Once an innovation is accepted by the market, Crown Cork & Seal selects the market segment in which it wants to compete and concentrates its R&D efforts on perfecting existing technology or hard-to-solve customer problems rather than on inventing new products.

As a final example, consider Compaq Computer. Exhibit 8.3 shows that Compaq spends less percentage wise on R&D than the other four firms listed. Compaq can be successful with such low relative R&D expenditures because it concentrates on integrating new technology (developed largely by other firms) into new products that give the customer a better value. It has also targeted a single segment of the computer industry on which to concentrate its efforts, the fast growing market for high performance desk top or portable computers. L. Perrigo, Crown Cork & Seal and Compaq all spend less percentage wise than the firms they compete with, yet all three are very successful in their chosen markets. They have selected an R&D strategy that is consistent with their corporate strategy, and don't even try (or want) to be on the leading edge of technology.

It is also possible to monitor technology in retailing. Sam Walton, founder of Wal-Mart Stores, spent almost as much time visiting the stores of his competitors, such as Fed-Mart and Kmart, as he did in his own stores. As he notes in his autobiography, many of his best ideas for Wal-Mart came from these visits to competitors' stores.[3]

3. A Middle Ground

General Electric and Caterpillar (formerly Caterpillar Tractor Company) are good examples of firms that fall in the middle ground between these two R&D strategies. Caterpillar spends most of its R&D funds on improving existing products. When it does bring out a new product, it is only after extensive testing and production of two months' supply of spare parts, and usually after another firm has developed and initially marketed the product. Firms such as General Electric and Caterpillar will typically spend 2–6% of their sales on R&D.

These three basic R&D strategies are summarized in Exhibit 8.4. A large firm engaged in multiple businesses such as General Electric may have divisional or product line R&D strategies. Such firms also need to decide whether R&D should be centralized, or whether each division should have its own R&D capability. Centralized control of R&D permits concentration of resources and scientific talent, as at Bell Telephone Laboratories, and makes it harder to hide projects from the scrutiny of top management. Decentralized, or divisional, control of R&D, as at Hewlett-Packard, makes R&D more responsive to the needs of a particular division. However, it is then more difficult to assemble enough resources in any one division for a major R&D effort.

---

3. Sam Walton, *Made in America: My Story* (New York: Doubleday, 1992), pp. 79–80.

R&D Expenditures	R&D as a % of Sales	Corporate Strategy	Examples
Low	<2%	Let someone else invent it and we will perfect it	Crown Cork & Seal (cans), Whirlpool (home appliances) Bandag (tire re-treading)
Medium	2–6%	Integrate technology into current products; keep abreast of competitors	GE (electronics, aerospace) Caterpillar (earth moving equipment)
High	7–12%	Steady innovation; constant stream of new products	Apple and Hewlett-Packard (computers) 3M (abrasives and coatings) Upjohn (pharmaceuticals)

Exhibit 8.4. R&D as a percent of sales and corporate strategies.

NEED FOR TOP MANAGEMENT SUPPORT

R&D does little good unless a corporation's top management will back what it develops. In the late 1970s, Xerox Corporation's Palo Alto Research Center (PARC) developed the major pieces of today's personal computer, namely a stand-alone desktop machine, the mouse, and the laser printer. However, Xerox top management thought the future lay in work stations linked to other pieces of Xerox office equipment and main frame computers. As a result, Xerox developed its work station, which never sold well. Then in the early 1980s, it abandoned PARC's efforts to make and market a personal computer. Shortly after, Apple Computer introduced its Macintosh, most of whose features had been developed at PARC. The Macintosh became an instant success, and Xerox shortly after left the computer business entirely.

Unless top management is willing to support the development of new products, it is likely an alert competitor will be the primary beneficiary of any technological breakthroughs.

RELATION TO PRODUCT LIFE CYCLE CONCEPT

These R&D strategies can be related to the product life cycle curve, as shown in Exhibit 8.5. The product life cycle curve represents the fact that products grow rapidly in their early years, plateau, then decline slowly. Innovative firms such as Hewlett-Packard and 3M depend upon a constant stream of new products for their continued growth. They also

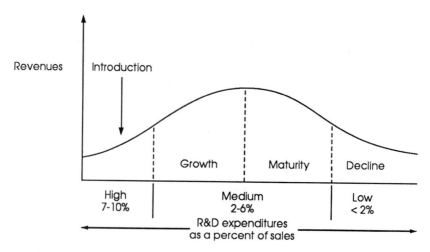

Exhibit 8.5. R&D as a percent of sales related to the product life cycle curve.

enjoy the high margins that are usually obtained during a product's rapid growth phase. Firms that monitor technology will wait to see which products look like they will be successful, then concentrate on perfecting or imitating them.

Little R&D money is spent on products that are well past the peak of the life cycle curve. These products open up another special strategy, that of replacement parts. Volume may be low, but so too are R&D costs, and margins are often higher than on new products which are subject to price cutting. The Bandag Corporation of Muscatine, Iowa is the world's leader in producing materials for the tire retreading industry. Its profitability figures are outstanding for any industry. In 1991 Bandag had a return on equity of 27 percent, virtually no long term debt, and an after tax return on sales of 13.7 percent. It also only spent 2.5% of sales on R&D.

The amount a firm should spend on R&D depends on its strategy. Two firms in the same industry can have very different strategies with respect to R&D, and yet both can be very successful (e.g., Compaq and Hewlett-Packard in computers). All firms need some capability in R&D, even if it is only to monitor the developments in technology to see what the potential impact will be on their firm. However, a strategy based on R&D innovation alone is not a guarantee of success. RC Companies (RC Cola) was the first to sell soft drinks in cans rather than the bottle, the first to have a diet (sugarless) soft drink (Diet Rite in 1960), and the first to have a caffeine-free soft drink (RC 100 in 1980). Yet it was not able to capitalize on any of these innovations. Coca-Cola and Pepsi-Cola (PepsiCo) both had vastly greater resources to spend on advertising (the real key to success in the soft drink business) and consequently were the firms that reaped the benefits of RC's innovations.

94

CREATIVITY AS R&D

Some firms have an ongoing need to make *different* products related to a common theme, rather than to make *better* products. Consider the toy and hobby industries, where creativity is the key to successful R&D. Firms that make toys need a steady stream of new products to remain successful. Their customers don't want to see the same products presented year after year. Here the thrust of research and development is to make a steady stream of different products, or to occasionally use new technology to make an old toy do something new, such as putting a miniature television camera in the cab of a toy train so the operator can see the track ahead just like the engineer on a real train would see it.

Because their product lines are always changing, toy makers may occasionally find themselves in the anomalous situation where their old (discontinued) models are in more demand than their new ones. Lionel trains are one of the best known American toys.[4] Their all metal trains from the 1950s often sell for five or more times their original price. Train sets from the 1930s and earlier in good condition sell at even higher premiums.

S-CURVES AND CORPORATE STRATEGY

R&D efforts can also have implications for corporate strategy in a given area of technology. The management consulting firm of McKinsey & Company has found that when performance is plotted as a function of cumulative development efforts (e.g., R&D man hours, R&D expenditures), an "S" shaped curve results, as shown in Exhibit 8.6.[5] The shape of the S-curve provides information about the expected results of additional developmental effort, a broad based term which includes research and development and all related activities. After a slow start (Point A in Exhibit 8.6), performance typically increases rapidly with increases in developmental effort (Point B), then slows to a halt (Point C).

S-curves have important implications for corporate strategy. First, if the S-curve for a particular technology has flattened out (e.g., for light bulbs), it is likely that competitors will soon match your performance, perhaps even exceed it if their plant and equipment is newer. This means your product has become a commodity and, unless you differentiate it in some way from the competitor's product, it will sell primarily on

---

4. For the history of the Lionel Train Company, see *All Aboard! The Story of Joshua Lionel Cowen and His Lionel Train Company* (New York: Workman Publishing Company, 1981).

5. Richard Foster, *Innovation: The Attacker's Advantage* (New York: Summit Books, 1986), Chapter 4.

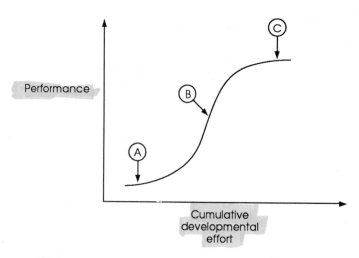

Exhibit 8.6. S-curve showing performance as a function of cumulative developmental effort.

the basis of price or delivery. The alternative is to develop a better product, such as fluorescent lighting for homes and offices or halogen headlights for automobiles.

Second, S-curves frequently occur in pairs, as shown in Exhibit 8.7. If your product offerings are based on technology represented by S_1, and you have been making these products for a long time (radios using vacuum tubes), you are likely near the performance limits of your technology (point L_1 in Exhibit 8.7). You need to be alert to competing products based on a new technology (transistorized radios) represented by S_2. Even though you may have a significant performance advantage over the new technology at T_1 (1960 for vacuum tube radios compared to transistorized ones), you need to watch carefully to see what the technological limits of the new technology appear to be. If they are significantly higher than the limits of your present technology, you will be at a disadvantage by time T_2 when the performance limits of the new technology will have surpassed those of the old (1970 for radios).

S-curves thus give rise to an important strategic question: when should a firm shift to a different technology (S-curve) to remain competitive or to survive? The answer is not always clear. Here are some questions to consider:

1. Is the new technology clearly superior? In the 1940s, makers of steam locomotives made great efforts to improve their products to be competitive with diesel powered locomotives, but the reality was that the diesel engine was so inherently superior that further production of steam locomotives could no longer be justified.

96

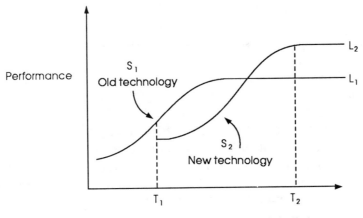

Exhibit 8.7. A pair of S-curves.

2. Will the cost of raw materials change? It may be possible to receive higher value from a technologically inferior product if its price is low enough. Thus copper is used to make electrical wire rather than gold, even though gold is a better conductor of electricity than copper.

3. Will there be another technological breakthrough soon? Perhaps we should plan to skip an S-curve. Rather than making radios with transistors instead of vacuum tubes, it might be to our advantage to wait a few years and make radios which use integrated circuits.

4. Do customers want the better product? The Polaroid SX-70 camera, introduced in 1972, was a quarter-inch thick, fold up marvel of technology that produced excellent color pictures. But customers apparently didn't care enough about getting their pictures instantly to pay a premium for the camera and the film. Kodak remained on its old S-curve (film that required separate processing) and was much more successful than Polaroid on its new S-curve.

5. Can we sell an old product on a new basis? By 1980 integrated circuits made it possible to purchase a watch with no moving parts that kept perfect time for less than $10. But that didn't make all traditional pin-lever (mechanical) watches obsolete. Rolex has been very successful selling its watches on the basis of status (advertisements by celebrities such as entertainer Bob Hope, opera singer Kiri Te Kanawa and fire fighter Red Adair in magazines such as *The New Yorker* and *Smithsonian*) and durability (one piece stainless steel or gold case). Rolex also felt that most of its potential customers did not particularly care if a watch kept *perfect* time so long as it kept

very good time (accuracy of a few seconds a day or a minute a week).[6] Further, some of Rolex's most popular watches have literally remained unchanged in appearance or construction for twenty years or more.

Examples of products that fit the S-curve analysis are given in Exhibit 8.8. Try to imagine new S-curves that might come into existence. Could newspapers be made obsolete by thin screen video displays that could take the place of a newspaper? Or could video cameras be developed which would take the place of standard cameras and film? Remember that in 1940 no one thought the thousands of steam locomotives then in service would be replaced *entirely* by the diesel locomotive by 1960. In 1950 almost no one even knew what a computer was. In 1960 no one who used a mainframe computer would have believed all that computing power could be contained in a personal computer that could sit on a desk and be used as easily at home as at work. And in 1970 no one thought a watch could be made for less than $5 that had no moving parts and kept perfect time. Yet we take all these achievements very matter of factly today.

The S-curve of many new technologies may not have significantly higher performance limits than those of existing technologies, but may offer other advantages. The 33 1/3 revolution per minute (rpm) long playing record was developed in 1948 by Peter Goldmark of CBS Laboratories, a division of CBS, Inc.[7] Over the next thirty years both reel to reel and cassette tape recorders were touted as better mediums for music than the long playing record, but in practice both were primarily used to complement, not replace, the long playing record. Then in the 1980s the compact disc (CD) became commercially available. Despite initially high prices of $1,000 or more per player and $20 or more per disc, CDs received an enthusiastic reception. CDs are often touted as offering distortion free music in contrast to records, which are inevitably subject to scratching and warping. But the real advantage of CDs compared to long playing records and tapes is their ease of use. It only takes seconds to program not only a sequence of discs but also individual entries on each disc.[8] (Each CD contains about the same amount of playing time as both

---

6. In 1926, a Rolex was the first wrist watch certified as an official chronometer, thereby indicating that wrist watches could keep time as accurately as the much larger pocket watches which men kept in a watch pocket. Shortly after timekeeping moved from one S-curve (pocket watches) to another (wrist watches).

7. Peter C. Goldmark, *Maverick Inventor* (New York: Saturday Review Press/E.P. Dutton & Company, 1973). See chapter 8, "The LP Caper, or the Case of the Missing Fuzz."

8. Several long playing records could be played in sequence using a record changer. However, since the records rested on each other, this inevitably caused wear and tear on the records. Also, only the top side of each record was played, making it necessary to physically turn the record over to hear both sides. Compact disc players come with magazines that can hold from five to twenty or more discs. The discs do not rest on each other, hence are subject to no more wear than if played one at a time. An entire magazine can be removed and replaced quickly and easily with another, thus permitting storage of compact discs in the magazine itself (records were stored individually in cardboard record cases) and grouped by music type (classical, country and western, popular). In the author's opinion, ease of use is the compact disc's real selling point.

Product	S1	S2	S3
Electronic amplifier	Vacuum tube	Transistor	Integrated circuit
Computation device	Abacus	Slide rule	Pocket calculator
Airplane engine	Piston	Jet	
Railroad locomotive	Steam	Diesel	
Watches	Pocket watch	Wrist watch	Solid state digital watch (no moving parts)
Tennis racket	Wood	Metal	Graphite
Skis	Wood	Aluminum	Fiberglass
Car tires	Rayon	Polyester	Radial
Television	Black & white	Color	Cable-ready (150+ channels)
Movies	At movie theater at scheduled times for a fee	At home on TV at scheduled time for free	At home on TV using VCR at viewer's convenience for small fee
Music reproduction	Long playing record	Tapes	Compact discs
Typing	Mechanical typewriter	Electric typewriter	Personal computer as word processor

Exhibit 8.8. S-curve analysis applied to selected products.

sides of a long playing record). When CDs were introduced in 1983, they accounted for just $17.2 million in sales. But by 1986, sales of CDs were $930 million, just slightly less than sales of long playing records. In 1991, sales of CDs reached $4.3 billion, while sales of long playing records fell to only $31 million. The CD has dramatically become the medium of choice for music lovers in just under ten years. This is no small achievement, since long playing records were the dominant means of playing music for almost forty years.

SUMMARY

A few products go on for decades with virtually no change, as is demonstrated by the examples of Hershey chocolate, Wrigley chewing gum and Rolex watches. But even a firm with a stable product line needs to be aware of what a shift to a new S-curve could do to its products. While innovation may be the order of the day in a few firms, most firms generally expect the life of their products to be several years or more. Indeed, most consumer products firms try to extend the life of their products indefinitely by developing them into well known brand names. Thus it is important for the general manager to consider possible S curves that may affect his business when formulating corporate strategy. If no major changes are in sight, then he can select the R&D strategy that is appropriate for his firm's products: innovation, monitoring technology, or a middle ground.

9

ORGANIZATIONAL STRUCTURE

All organizations have an organizational structure, although in some cases it is much more formal than in others. In most small firms the structure is quite informal. But by the time a firm grows to Fortune 500 size, it has almost always developed a formal structure which is displayed as the firm's organization chart. While strategy and structure have always been closely related, business historian Alfred Chandler was the first to study this relationship in depth through case studies of businesses such as General Motors and Sears Roebuck and Company.[1] Chandler drew the conclusion that structure follows strategy, but subsequent studies have indicated that the relationship is not always that straightforward. What is clear is that the general manager needs to have an understanding of the three basic types of organizational structure and the advantages and disadvantages of each.

Historically there have been two basic forms of organizational structure: the purely *functional* organization and the *line and staff* organization.[2] Since the 1960s a third type of organizational structure, called the *matrix*, has attracted considerable attention.

THE FUNCTIONAL STRUCTURE

Virtually all businesses start off with a functional structure. This means that directly under the president there is an individual in charge of each

1. Alfred D. Chandler, Jr., *Strategy and Structure: Chapters in the History of Industrial Enterprise* (Cambridge, MA: MIT Press, 1962).

2. General Motors, long the largest manufacturing firm in the world, is generally considered to be the first firm to develop and use the line and staff form of structure in an industrial setting. Peter F. Drucker described the General Motors system of management in his *Concept of the Corporation* (New York: Harper & Row, 1947) and gave it a name, "decentralization." Shortly thereafter, under the direction of Ralph Cordiner, General Electric also adopted decentralized management, and by the mid-1950s it was widely accepted as the best way to manage a large corporation.

major functional area (accounting, production, sales). A typical organizational chart for a functional organization is shown in Exhibit 9.1. The functional organization works well for small companies or individual plants.[3] However, once a firm takes on multiple products and multiple locations to produce those products, the functional organization runs into difficulties with communication and control. All decisions regarding a functional area are assumed to be made at corporate headquarters by the person who is the head of the appropriate functional area. This can cause delays in getting timely answers to problems at the plant level and hinders coordination (horizontal communication) between plants. It also removes the decision making from the level at which the decision will be implemented. Those at the plant level who know (and care) the most about the problem only provide information to those higher up, and have little if any direct input into decisions that affect them.

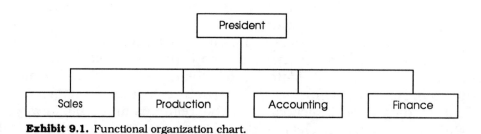

Exhibit 9.1. Functional organization chart.

THE LINE AND STAFF STRUCTURE

The most common solution to the problems of communication and detached decision making caused by the functional organizational structure is the shift to a line and staff organization. Roughly modeled after the military, the line and staff organizational structure provides for one individual to be in control (i.e., have authority to make decisions within preestablished limits) at each operating unit. Essentially it provides for a plant (general) manager at the local level. The line organization is represented by solid lines on the organizational chart, as shown in Exhibit 9.2. Overlaid on this chart are dotted lines representing functional lines of authority or expertise in staff functions such as finance and accounting.

---

3. Occasionally a billion dollar corporation will use the purely functional form of organization. In the 1950s Crown Cork and Seal under John F. Connelly scrapped its decentralized form of organizational structure and put a purely functional form in its place that remains to this date. Crown has been one of the most successful firms in its industry (can production, canning machinery, bottle caps). But large firms using a functional organizational structure are exceptions to the norm, and much of the credit in Crown's case must go to Mr. Connelly, its chairman, who made responsiveness to customer needs a core value at Crown.

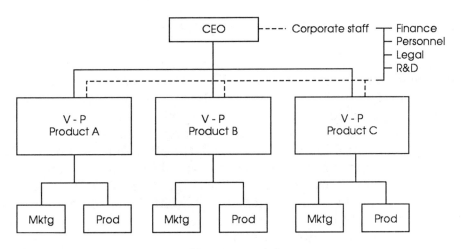

Exhibit 9.2. Typical line and staff organizational chart.

This structure provides both a source of expertise and a degree of corporate-wide standardization for such functions as accounting, purchasing, styling and research and development. Plant (or branch) managers have considerable discretion to make decisions (and products) within broad-based corporate guidelines. General Motors is a classic example, where the division managers of Cadillac, Buick, Oldsmobile, Pontiac and Chevrolet have responsibility for product planning subject to corporate guidelines that the hierarchy of models will range from Chevrolet at the bottom end to Cadillac at the top. Features initially introduced on a Cadillac (power steering, air conditioning) are introduced sequentially throughout the other models in subsequent years. The line and staff form of organization is best suited to corporations with several divisions, each with standardized products or services with high volume.

Both the functional and line and staff forms of organization have implicit in them the concept that each manager has one and only one superior, much like the chain of command in the military. While this makes sense in most manufacturing and service businesses, it has disadvantages in organizations which by their knowledge intensive nature make frequent use of project teams or highly skilled professionals (accountants, consultants, engineers). Such firms rarely have high volume production or standardized output. Instead of organizing for mass production, these firms commonly group professionals together to work on projects on a temporary basis. These professionals are customarily placed under the direction of a project manager who, as the title indicates, is the link to the line organization and is responsible for completing the projects on time and within budget.

THE MATRIX STRUCTURE

Project organizations are the best known form of the *matrix organization.* The distinguishing characteristic of a matrix organization is that by design an employee has two individuals to whom he reports: his home (functional) department head and his project manager, as shown in Exhibit 9.3. The advantage of the matrix organization is that it permits assembling considerable expertise under the direction of a single individual (the project manager) who has responsibility for the entire project. Matrix organizations have been used with great success by research and development intensive firms such as Hewlett-Packard (computers) and Upjohn (pharmaceutical products) to develop new products. Once the product reaches the production stage, the project team (or task force, as it is sometimes called) is usually dissolved and its members either returned to their home departments or assigned to another project.

The disadvantage of the matrix organization usually comes from the point of view of the individual. He has to please two bosses at once, and it may not be clear which one really has the power to control his rewards or advancement opportunities in the company.[4] A second disadvantage comes from the possibility of "negative mind set" on the part of the department manager responsible for a group of individuals assigned to project teams. If this manager competes with the individual project managers and tries to manipulate the assignment of individuals to project teams to his own advantage, the results are likely to be counterproductive for the projects and for the organization as a whole. For the

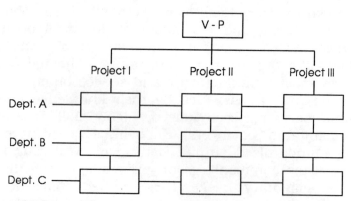

Exhibit 9.3. The matrix organizational structure.

---

4. For a discussion of some of the challenges of using or working in a matrix organization, see Harvey F. Kolodny, "Managing in a Matrix," *Business Horizons*, March-April 1981, pp. 17–24.

matrix organization to be successful, there must be shared resources, mutual trust and confidence, a sense of team play, and a willingness to put the good of the project ahead of individual accomplishments. Needless to say, it is difficult to find highly trained individuals who possess all these attributes. Such individuals are usually high achievers who have been rewarded for individual accomplishment (e.g., high grades, advanced degrees) rather than cooperative or team effort, and may find it frustrating to subordinate personal desires to project needs.

The matrix organization described to this point is designed to concentrate technically capable resources so they can solve a problem or complete a project. Even if individuals aren't of the same background (all electrical engineers), they have a common focus and a common interest. There is a second and probably more common, if less well publicized, form of the matrix organization. It is used when there is a need to provide a variety of expert services locally in several different functions over a geographically dispersed area, but the need for expertise isn't large enough to merit a separate facility staffed by individuals each with a specific expertise.

In such situations, the matrix organization is used to provide an administrative chain of command whose purpose is to support locally assigned technical experts who receive their tasking directly from headquarters. As shown in Exhibit 9.4, there are regional offices with an administrative head who reports directly to headquarters. In each of these regional offices there are experts in a set of functional areas who report for administrative purposes only to the office manager, and who report for purposes of work assignments and technical direction to a functional expert on the headquarters staff. Depending on the size of the

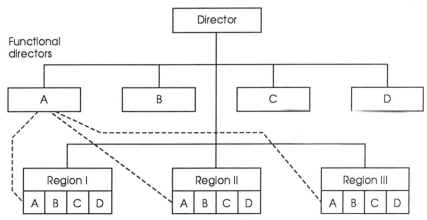

Exhibit 9.4. Matrix organization to provide administrative support to geographically dispersed locations.

organization, local offices may report to district offices which in turn report to regional offices. A structure similar to this is used by the Department of Natural Resources (DNR) in the state of Michigan, which has its headquarters in Lansing but must provide specialized services concerning preservation and use of natural resources throughout the entire state. The U.S. Navy uses a similar arrangement whereby the commanding officer of a ship is responsible for operations to an *operational* commander, but receives direction and support from his *type* commander's staff officers who are expert in such areas as administration, weapons, supply or engineering. In fact, most people in large organizations that are spread over vast geographic regions will work to some extent in this form of matrix organization.

WHAT STRUCTURE IS APPROPRIATE?

Most firms will naturally evolve toward the organizational structure that is appropriate for their business. Almost all small firms use a simple functional structure. Large manufacturing firms use decentralized management and the line and staff form of organization. Firms that innovate constantly or work for many different clients use the matrix form. For successful consumer product firms, there is a fairly predictable cycle in the development of their organizational structures. Many large firms (IBM, Xerox) are essentially marketing firms with a single or related line of products (computers, copiers, typewriters, word processors). These firms progress from a functional organization at the beginning through a product oriented structure (much like the line and staff organization used by General Motors) as they add new products. Then as they get larger, they are more likely to return to their original functional structure, as shown in Exhibit 9.5.

Apple computer is an excellent example.[5] After its initial success with the Apple series of computers, it developed, manufactured and sold its Macintosh computer as a separate product line. Indeed, even the facilities used for the Macintosh were physically separate from the ones used to produce the original product, the Apple II series of personal computers. Its organizational structure then looked as shown in Exhibit 9.6. The problem with this structure was that the Apple Division made most of the money, but took a back seat as far as corporate interest and attention goes, primarily from the firm's founder and then president, Steven Jobs. Shortly after John Sculley came to Apple

---

5. "Apple's New Crusade," *Business Week*, November 26, 1984, p. 146 and *The Wall Street Journal*, June 3, 1985, p. 2.

Computer in 1983 from PepsiCo to bring some marketing expertise to the firm, he reorganized Apple along functional lines, as shown in Exhibit 9.7. The functional structure has the following advantages:

1. it eliminates duplication of effort at each division.
2. it reduces the chances of favoritism being shown to one division over another
3. it brings all R&D personnel together under a common superior, even though they may actually work at physically separated facilities where individual products are made.
4. advertising campaigns can be coordinated across product lines.
5. sales territory assignments can be more easily coordinated to prevent duplicate calls by salesmen from different divisions on the same customer.

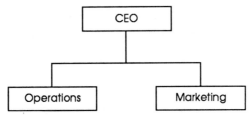

Exhibit 9.5. Simplified functional organizational structure.

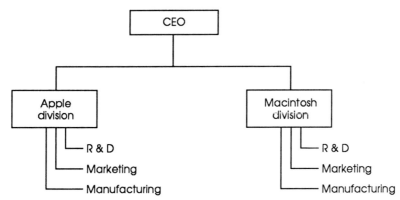

Exhibit 9.6. Organizational structure of Apple Computer after development of the Macintosh.

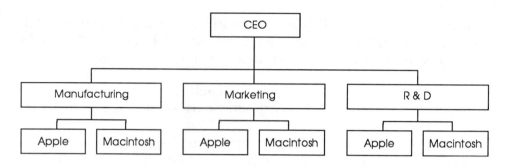

Exhibit 9.7. Organizational structure of Apple Computer after its reorganization in 1983.

Because of these advantages, this form of functional structure is used by most large organizations, especially those making consumer goods, where the key skill is marketing.

There is also a disadvantage to the functional organizational structure. When divisions lose their autonomy, they also tend to lose the pride they had in being a separate unit (e.g., the former Macintosh development group at Apple Computer). But for most firms with related consumer goods products, the advantages of the functional organizational structure usually outweigh the disadvantages. General guidelines for selecting an organizational structure are summarized in Exhibit 9.8.

Type of Business	Organizational Structure
Small business, single product firm	Functional
Multi-product manufacturing firm (General Motors, General Electric)	Line and staff
Large related product consumer goods firm (IBM, Procter & Gamble)	Functional
Continuous innovation, many new products (3M, Hewlett-Packard)	Matrix for R&D and product development
Geographically dispersed over a large area (military, state agencies)	Functional for operations, matrix to provide administrative support

Exhibit 9.8. Guidelines for selecting an organizational structure.

Summary

The general manager should select the structure that best fits his or her own organization's situation, making allowance for any unusual or unique circumstances. The functional organization tends to be better for firms that need to coordinate related product lines (office equipment, apparel) over a wide geographic area. The line and staff organization tends to be better for manufacturing firms that want to make and market several product lines independently (home appliances, jet engines, financial services). Finally, it may be desirable to use different structures in different parts of the organization. Thus R&D may use a matrix organization to facilitate the development of new products while manufacturing and marketing may use a functional organization to facilitate production and sales of the company's products.

━ 10 ━

CONCLUDING REMARKS

This has been a book about what the general manager should know about the formulation of strategy in business organizations. It recognizes that strategy formulation is, and always will be, as much an art as it is a science. Like the artist, the strategist needs some general rules to follow, and should strive to learn from the experiences of others. Otherwise his or her efforts at formulating strategy are virtually certain to end in failure.

Some individuals seem to have a natural understanding of the nature of strategic decisions while others have to work hard to develop this perspective. The five step strategic planning framework discussed in Chapter 3 is a good starting point for all problems in strategy formulation. Consider now Kmart and Hot 'N' Now, both classic examples of clearly formulated corporate strategy.

THE KMART EXAMPLE

Until the early 1950s, the S. S. Kresge Company of Detroit and its larger rival, the F. W. Woolworth Company, headquartered in New York City, dominated the low priced retail market. Both had stores centrally located in virtually every city and large town in the country. Both offered personal service and an enormous variety of low priced goods. However, by the mid-1950s, Kresge's sales had stagnated and profits were starting to decline. Harry B. Cunningham, soon to become president of S. S. Kresge, spent nearly two years traveling the country to see what could be done to stimulate sales and increase earnings.

On his travels, he observed that large cities such as Detroit were losing population, particularly their increasingly affluent middle class, to the suburbs.[1] At the same time, wage rates were rising, making personal selling in stores more expensive. Finally, Cunningham noted that higher priced consumer items such as home appliances, television

1. In 1950, Detroit's population was 1,849,000. By 1985 it had fallen forty percent to 1,077,000.

sets and auto parts provided higher profits than the traditional items carried in a five and dime store.

He proposed a radical shift in strategy to Kresge's board of directors: open large new stores in affluent suburban areas and close all S. S. Kresge dime stores that were not profitable. These new stores, to be called Kmarts, would continue to offer much of what the S. S. Kresge stores offered. However, they would also sell higher priced, brand name consumer durables at discounted prices. All products would be available through self-service, and check out counter personnel would be paid the minimum wage or slightly more to keep labor costs down.

The first Kmart opened in 1962 in a Detroit suburb (Garden City) and was an immediate success. Kresge's sales and earnings grew rapidly, and in 1977 the company changed its name to Kmart Corporation. In 1987, Kmart sold its remaining 57 S. S. Kresge stores to McCrory Corporation. By the end of 1988, there were 2,243 Kmart stores. The Kmart story is a clear example of how a successful strategy can be developed in response to changes in the economy and society as a whole. Kmart's primary competitor, F. W. Woolworth, did not change its strategy until a decade later. Kmart, meantime, passed Woolworth is sales in 1970 to become the nation's second largest retailer behind Sears, Roebuck and Company.

THE HOT 'N' NOW EXAMPLE

A more recent success story is that of William Van Domelen and the Hot 'N' Now fast food chain. In the early 1980s, while he owned several Wendy's franchises in western Michigan, Van Domelen noticed that all the major fast food franchises, including industry leader McDonald's, were raising prices to cover the cost of their expanded menus and refurnished facilities. Van Domelen saw an opportunity to return to the initial McDonald's strategy of offering a limited fast food menu served quickly and sold at prices below those of the competition.

Van Domelen believed so much in this concept that he sold his Wendy's franchises to pursue it. He opened his first Hot 'N' Now restaurant in Kalamazoo, Michigan, in 1985. His strategy had three major goals:

- sell for less than the competition. This was the origin of the thirty-nine cent Hot 'N' Now hamburger, which still sells at that price.
- have the fastest service time in the business
- get the order right every time.

The simple menu (limited to hamburgers, french fries and a soft drink) facilitates achievement of all three of these goals. The concept was an immediate success, and by 1990 there were 71 Hot 'N' Now fast food restaurants in the midwest and sunbelt states. In December 1990, Taco Bell, a subsidiary of PepsiCo, acquired the Hot 'N' Now chain from Van Domelen with the intention of expanding it nationwide.

LEARNING ABOUT STRATEGY

Young managers rarely get an opportunity to formulate and implement a strategy. Major strategic decisions probably only occur once every five to ten years in most corporations and are made by a handful of people, usually the board of directors and the senior officers. While reading is no substitute for experience, we can learn much from books on strategy and biographies of people who have been involved in major strategic decisions. We can also learn a great deal about "real time" strategy decisions by reading *The Wall Street Journal* and business periodicals such as *Business Week*, *Financial World* and *Fortune*.

We can also learn much by being observant when we go shopping or travel. What products are people buying or using? Why has the price of some items increased and of others decreased? What new buildings are going up and what sorts of businesses will they house? Are businesses locating downtown or in the suburbs? Such observations can help us pinpoint trends and new developments in technology, just as they helped Harry B. Cunningham in reformulating S. S. Kresge's strategy and William Van Domelen in envisioning the concept of the Hot 'N' Now fast food restaurants. In fact, one of the most enjoyable aspects of strategic planning is that in one way or another almost everything we do has some bearing on it.

FURTHER READING

The following books provide good insights into the process of formulating strategy.

Andrews, Kenneth R., *The Concept of Corporate Strategy* (third edition). Homewood, IL: Richard D. Irwin, 1987.

Classic Harvard Business School approach to strategy.

Ansoff, Igor H., *Corporate Strategy*. New York: McGraw-Hill, 1965.

An original and still useful discussion of business strategy.

Drucker, Peter F., *The Practice of Management*. New York: Harper & Row, 1954.

The classic discussion of the tasks of the general manager.

Ohmae, Kenichi, *The Mind of the Strategist*. New York: McGraw-Hill, 1982.

Explains how the Japanese have segmented markets with great success.

Peters, Thomas J. and Robert H. Waterman, Jr., *In Search of Excellence: Lessons from America's Best Run Firms*. New York: Harper & Row, 1982.

This all time best-seller gives good examples of some well run American firms. It includes an emphasis on quality which the authors feel was lacking in many American firms. Chapter 2 also tells what the authors think was wrong with American business schools at the time of the book's writing. Focuses on the customer, where *Marketing Warfare* (see below) focuses on the competition.

Trout, Jack, and Al Ries, *Marketing Warfare*. New York: McGraw-Hill, 1985.

Compares business to warfare, but is most useful for its simple framework of the proper competitive action to take given a firm's position in its industry. Focuses on the competition, where *In Search of Excellence* focuses on the customer.

Porter, Michael, *Competitive Strategy: Techniques for Analyzing Industries and Competitors*. New York: The Free Press, 1980.

Stresses competition within an industry and between firms in that industry.

Autobiographies and biographies of individuals who have been involved in making major strategic decisions also make worthwhile reading. The following are but a few of the many excellent autobiographies and biographies of business leaders available. Although they worked in a wide variety of industries, they shared the common perspective of the general manager.

Collier, Peter, and David Horowitz, *The Fords: An American Epic.* New York: Summit Books, 1987.

A fascinating look at the Ford family and the Ford Motor Company, from Henry Ford through his grandson, Henry Ford II.

Kurtzig, Sandra L., *CEO: Building a $400 Million Company from the Ground Up.* New York: W. W. Norton, 1991.

About starting and building a computer software firm, including taking it public.

Love, John F., *McDonald's: Behind the Arches.* New York: Bantam Books, 1986.

This tells the story not only of Ray Kroc and the founding of McDonald's but of the development of the fast food industry as well.

Montgomery, M. R., *In Search of L. L. Bean.* Boston: Little, Brown and Company, 1985.

How L. L. Bean and Company became the famous mail order firm.

Ogilvy, David, *Confessions of an Advertising Man.* New York: Atheneum, 1966.

The story of the Ogilvy & Mather advertising agency, but also good insights, particularly into the importance and proper use of advertising, useful in any business or organization.

Sloan, Alfred P., Jr., *My Years at General Motors.* New York: Doubleday and Company, 1963.

The development of General Motors and the automobile business from the point of view of the man often credited with developing the system of management used so successfully by General Motors.

Walton, Sam, *Made in America: My Story.* New York: Doubleday, 1992.

How Sam Walton made Wal-Mart Stores the nation's largest retailer, in his own words.

Watson, Thomas J., Jr., *A Business and Its Beliefs: The Ideas that Helped Build IBM.* New York: McGraw-Hill, 1963.

Probably the best known and most quoted of the McKinsey Foundation Lecture Series given annually since 1955 by an outstanding business leader at the Graduate School of Business at Columbia University.

INDEX

Ten Largest U.S. Retailers, 1991

		Sales*	Net Income*	—Return on—		Employees
				Sales	Equity	
1	Sears Roebuck	$ 57,242	$1,279	2.2%	9.2%	450,000
2	Wal-Mart Stores	43,887	1,609	3.7%	23.0%	364,000
3	Kmart	34,969	859	2.5%	14.5%	348,000
4	Kroger	21,351	80	0.4%	n/a#	170,000
5	American Stores	20,100	199	1.0%	13.3%	148,000
6	J.C. Penney	17,295	80	0.5%	1.1%	185,000
7	Dayton Hudson	16,115	301	1.9%	12.4%	157,000
8	Safeway	15,119	55	0.4%	25.6%	110,064
9	A&P	11,391	151	1.3%	12.4%	99,300
10	May Department Store	10,615	515	4.9%	17.9%	115,000
	Totals:	$248,084	$5,128			2,146,364

*Sales and Net Income figures in millions of dollars
Company has negative shareholders' equity

Selected other figures for Fortune's 50 largest retailers:

Median return on equity:	13.6%
Median return on sales:	2.1%
Median return on assets:	3.2%
Average assets to sales:	.64
Average sales per employee:	$110,589

Adapted from *Fortune*, June 1, 1992, pp. 188–189